Power for Living

By the same author

Healing Revolution
Healing Secrets
Radiant Christian Living
The Greatest Miracle

Forthcoming title:
God's Marvels – Melvin Banks brings his own extraordinary story up-to-date in this power-packed new title. To be published in summer 1990.

Rev. Melvin Banks would be pleased to hear from readers.Please write to him at:
 Crusade Office
 44 Monk's Way
 Cricketts Meadow
 Chippenham
 Wilts
 SN15 3TT

(Please send s.a.e)

Tel. 0249–655712

Power for Living

Making the most of your life in Christ

**Melvin Banks
With
Jenny Roberts**

Marshall Pickering

Marshall Morgan and Scott
Marshall Pickering
34 – 42 Cleveland Street, London, W1P 5FB. U.K.

Copyright © 1989 Melvin Banks
First published in 1989 by Marshall Morgan and Scott Publications Ltd
Part of the Marshall Pickering Holdings Group

British Library Cataloguing in Publication Data
Power for Living.
1. Christian life
248.4

ISBN 0-551-01881-X

Text Set in Bembo by Selectmove
Printed and bound in Great Britain by
Courier International Ltd, Tiptree, Essex

ACKNOWLEDGEMENTS

Happy the man, and happy he alone,
He who can call today his own,
He who, secure within, can say:
Tomorrow do thy worst,
For I have lived today. . .

John Dryden

I thank God for those who have helped me to live the full life, thus so far and have shared the journey with me, in introducing thousands to Christ all over Europe and across the world, in my 35 years in preaching the Word of God.

I thank my wonderful wife Lilian, who is incredibly beautiful, and so easy to live with!; a marvellous mother who gave me the foundation stones of life; two good sons, who inspire me, and great team members like Brian Hilleard, John Whitehouse, Roland Parsons, John Bryant, David Hill, Bruce Kent, Joe Holly, Freddie Gallichan, Maurice Cowling . . . and so many others . . . Thank you all.

Above all thanks to Jesus our Lord and Saviour, who reminds us:

The words that I give you are spirit and life

Contents

I: *What is life?*

I remember singing as a young lad 'There is life for a look at the crucified one'. I often got mixed up with the second lines (I never was much of a singer when I sang in the local Salvation Army Songsters!) and added incorrectly 'There is life full, rich and free. . .' The words may not have been part of the song, but I have found them to be true. And as I have walked the dark cloisters of this world, campaigning and preaching the Gospel, bringing health and healing to so many from Singapore to New Delhi, from Zululand to the outback of the Australian bush, from the most southerly towns of the world deep in the South Island of New Zealand to John O'Groats in northern Scotland, everywhere I have found people longing for LIFE.

When Hagar and Ishmael in the desert found their bottle was empty and water was miraculously supplied (Genesis 14), Ishmael was not taken out of the wilderness, but grew up in that dry, barren land. He became an archer (a victor, a conqueror, a winner), and 'God was with the lad'. He was given a well – an everlasting supply of fresh water.

God does not offer us mere escapism or fantasy. He does not remove us from the problems of this world, but gives us a life of fulfilment and achievement in the midst of it. In a world full of the grim reality of selfishness, war, division, blasphemy, suffering, tension,. . . we can be *full of life* in the midst of it all!

A ship encountered great difficulty on a long voyage, and the supply of drinking water ran out. The passengers and crew were becoming desperate, and the sight of so much undrinkable water around was almost too much to bear. In utter desperation, the story goes, a passenger lowered a bucket into the ocean, scooped seawater on board, and despite the inevitable consequences begun to gulp down the water. No one was more surprised than he to discover that the water was pure – it had not even a taste of salt – and before long everybody was enjoying the curious phenomenon.

Later, investigations revealed that the ship had sailed into water from a huge freshwater river, and the strong current had caused the clean water to wash into the ocean, pressing back the briny surf! In the midst of the impure and life-threatening environment, there was a pocket of fresh, thirst-quenching, reviving, life-sustaining water!

Is life worth living? We live in the midst of a dying, decaying, decadent, lost, corrupt, soul-destroying society. Each year over 18,000 people in the United States come to the conclusion that life isn't worth living. Some take poison, others jump from bridges or apartment houses, while others resort to firearms. Are these people right? Is life worth living after all?

Life is *not* worth living if you live it only for *fortune*. Jay Gould, the multi-millionaire, said, 'I am the most miserable man on this earth.' Ivan Krueger, wealthy head of the world's largest monopoly, committed suicide.

Or if you live it only for *fame*. 'I walk up and down thinking I am happy and knowing I am not,' said the famous essayist, Charles Lamb. Stephen Foster, composer of 'Old Black Joe', 'Swannee River' and other plantation songs, died a drunkard's death at the age of 38. Edgar Allan Poe drank himself to death.

Or if we live it only for *power*. Napoleon died a lonely horrible death on the island where he was exiled. Julius Caesar was assassinated. Mussolini was executed.

Or if we live only for *pleasure*. After years of pleasure, Robert Burns wrote: 'Pleasures are as poppies spread, you seize the flower, the bloom is shed.' Lord Byron, who lived a life of sinful pleasure, lived and died an unhappy man.

But life *is* worth living if you live it *for Christ*. The educated apostle Paul wrote, 'For me to live is Christ, and to die is gain'. The uneducated Jerry McAuley, 'the river thief', found such joy in living after he started to live for Christ that he established rescue missions to tell others the good news that life is worth living when it's lived for Jesus. Yes, from all walks of life, people have found that a life for Christ is a life of joy.

How does Christ make life worth living?

First, he forgives all your sinful past. As long as your past sins are bothering you, a joyous life is impossible.

Second, he gives hope and help for the present. 'My God shall supply all your needs according to his riches in glory by Christ Jesus' (Philippians 4:19).

Third, Christ promises you everlasting life and an eternal home. 'As many as received him [Christ], to them he gave power to become the sons of God' (John 1:12).

This Christ who can save you from eternal death and make your life worth living asks only one thing – obedience to him.

In the midst of all man's troubles – is life worth living? There is a current of fresh vibrating power that can not only, *keep you alive*, but *give you life*—in Jesus' words, 'more abundantly'.

Jesus came to give us that life. This is why most people miss life, because they hunt for it in the devices of men and the traditions of time. Our great enemy came to 'kill, and destroy. . .' but on Calvary Jesus Christ broke the serpent's back. He won for us the ultimate declaration of victory. But it still awaits applicants to enjoy its mighty outworking.

He wants to pour this life into us. Calvary's price is Calvary's power. This is the mystery of Calvary, the paradox that our life, born in Christ's death and his sacrificial giving, becomes a worship, a joy to his heart. . . that we have found life through him.

This is why this powerful, all-absorbing, all-sufficient message deeply satisfies and affects every part of our lives, including the most simple and practical details. Here is the answer to boredom, what to do when fatigued, how to find continuous enthusiasm, keep a sense of simple wonder and joy handle stress successfully.

It is the secret of living life to the full. **Power for Living!**

The Rev Melvin Banks
Crusade Office
44 Monk's Way
Cricketts Meadow
Chippenham
Wiltshire SN15 3TT
England

II: *Discovering Life*

A friend introduced me to an enthusiastic young man at the end of a campaign meeting in a cinema in New Zealand. Bright eyed and radiantly happy, he told me of his conversion the year before and described his previous life. He had drunk heavily and lost one position after another, each job further down the economic scale. Finally he was distraught with trouble, his live-in girlfriend was pregnant, and he shuffled through the streets from town to town, dirty, unshaven, broke, defeated, sleeping at times in haystacks, barns and alleys. Then he fell into the drugs scene. First he carried drugs from one town to another, then slowly elevated himself financially through this risky business—for in New Zealand, as elsewhere, it is a heavily punished offence. He finally became a drug pusher, earning huge amounts of money, moved to a large city, and found himself a luxurious flat.

One day his new landlord came to collect the rent, and the conversation took a surprising turn.

'My wife has complained for years of pain in her spine,' the landlord remarked. 'She can't bend to reach things, she's doubled up in the mornings, and has suffered like this for donkeys' years. Doctors can't help – their pills soon wear off and she's back where she started.

'Me, I'm not religious,' he said sceptically. 'When she said she was going to one of these healing things—some service in a cinema in town—I laughed at her. I thought she'd gone scatty. But some of her friends had been and said it was marvellous, so off she went. But d'you know,' he said more philosophically, 'it jolly well did the trick, by jumping kiwis it worked!'

Chuckling, he added, 'You could have knocked me down with a banana when she came waltzing in, touched her toes and did a dance round the front room. Marvellous! I'm going down to see what it's like tonight.'

Bemused, he walked off, and then turned back. He had forgotten to pick up the rent!

Young Gary thought; this is really strange! He'd never seen the landlord go away without the rent, let alone anyone captured by religion! In a cinema, did he say? Miracles? 'I'd never believed in anything myself, but this had to be worth having a look at. And it's *free?*'

The next night Gary went along to the meeting. He found people queuing up on the main street of the town to go into the cinema. Large posters advertised myself and the team for the 'Miracle Healing Services'. He thought, 'I've never heard of anyone queuing up to go into a religious service before.' It was packed with over 1,000 people but he got a seat near the back.

Gary went on with his story, describing the worship and the lively dancing before the Lord. Folk doing a 'jig' in church was something to watch indeed! The happiness on hundreds of faces, the unbelievable joyous atmosphere—it was marvellous! He heard me preach a simple message of faith, he told me. He had never thought about personal faith before, and was captivated. He felt the power of God touch his life as he heard the words of the Bible, and he was changed on the spot. He was later counselled by an experienced Christian helper, but he said it was in his seat that God broke him, melted him, showed him his awful sins and redeemed him. He became a new creation. 'I felt I wasn't the same man.'

There he was, as I visited the cinema again twelve months later, a well-dressed, happy, quietly spoken eager young fellow. He had not missed one church service in a year, and he was there as soon as the doors were open each night. He had married the young lady he had been living with, she had become converted, they had a little child and they worshipped as a family together.

I asked him about the drug pushing, and he explained that he had gone home and flushed them all down the toilet and had given up all drug-taking that very day. He had since found a good job.

As he spoke he clutched a New Testament which looked tattered and worn. He had been given it new by a local church a day or two after his amazing conversion. He had read it through twelve times and its message had penetrated his life, enabling him to get in harmony with God. Faith arising from that Word had lifted him in a year from a pigmy of doubt into a giant of faith, a great soul winner—he had won many others to Christ. As he believed the message of God, faith-power had been unlocked. He had learnt to pray and to practise the life of Christ. He had discovered the importance of bridling his tongue, found the answer to stress, been lost in the wonder of awe, worship, praise; he knew the power it gives to unlock your faith, the vital importance of dethroning self, of surrendering the thought life.

After finishing his remarkable story, he thanked me for revealing the power of God to him. 'I discovered what life was that night,' he went on. '*I came alive*, and through the teaching of Jesus, I have found how to *keep fully alive ever since*.'

His last words burnt in my mind, and I chewed them over. How many people need to know how to keep alive all through life. I determined to make these truths even more widely known.

The man sat with head down at the close of a crowded service in the north of England. His world had collapsed. His wife had suddenly died, he had struggled to bring up his children, nothing had gone right, and after years of relative happiness and prosperity he had lost everything.

'It's all right for you preachers,' he said, 'you don't have any real problems!' How mistaken he was, because I hear nothing but peoples problems from morning to night almost every day of my life.

Then this big man sobbed like a child and and blurted out, 'You are so happy, Reverend Banks, show me how to start *living again*.'

The challenge of that sobbing voice tugged at my heart, and what I taught that man that day, and have included in my preaching and counselling ever since, has brought me tens of thousands of letters of thanks and appreciation over many years.

When asked by a minister 'Are you afraid to die?' One man replied, 'No, sir, but I am afraid to live.' People are dying all round us. They want to know how to get through today, and see their way through next week.

Someone spelt out the recent turbulent decades in this way:

> the Trapped 1920s
> the Trying 1930s
> the Fearful 1940s
> the Frantic 1950s
> the Sad 1960s
> the Chronic 1970s
> the Violent 1980s

People have become fragmented, dispirited, misdirected. And what of the 1990s?

Solomon spoke long ago for empty, hollow, wandering man: 'I looked at everything I had tried, it was all so useless, a chasing of the wind, and there was nothing really worthwhile anywhere. . .' (Ecclesiastes 2: 11, Living Bible).

A doctor described most peoples's way of life as 'death on the instalment plan'!

Charles Dickens' words in his *Pickwick Papers* 140 years ago, could be for today: 'the tired sad expressions, the care-worn faces, the dormant affections, the heartless eye that no longer glints. . .'

Man's problems and pressures abound and pile upon him. William Wordsworth so aptly expressed man's uncertainty, fears, listlessness, emptiness, and lack of determination in the words of his poem

'The affliction of Margaret'.

> My apprehensions come in crowds;
> I dread the rustling of the grass;

The very shadows of the clouds
Have power to shake me as they pass,
I question things, and do not find
One that will answer to my mind;
And all the world appears unkind.

Beyond participation lie
My troubles, and beyond relief:
Pity me and not my grief,
Come to me, my son, or send some
Tidings, that my woes may end;
I have no earthly friend . . .

There is a story about a great jet flying across America at 40,000 feet, totally by automatic pilot. The voice came on: 'This is a recording. You have the privilege of flying in the first flight by a totally electronic jet. It took off electronically from Chicago, it is flying electronically, it will land at Los Angeles electronically. This plane has no pilot, no co-pilot, no flight engineer. Do not worry nothing can go wrong, nothing I repeat can go wrong. . . can go wrong. . . can go wrong . . .go wrong, wrong, wrong, wrong. . .'

But there *is* something wrong with our scientific, educated, sophisticated, electronically technical age.

The emphasis today is on living. People want life! TV, radio, billboards, newspaper advertising, all offer us cigarettes, alcohol, holidays in exotic places. . .you need this perfume, this deodorant, and if your world is falling about you, just sit back and take a cigar and everything will come out all right! We are told that 'Coke adds life,' and that if you use this hairspray, ladies, handsome young men will come running after you and enrich your life! Advertising is capitalising on man's great quest for fulfilment, happiness an health.

What Liberace the famous pianist said is true. After earning £400 million in his lifetime (he even had a piano in his swimming pool), he confessed he did not have *life*, and said dejectedly just before he died in abject misery, 'To have health and contentment is life.'

9

Behind the tawdry actors of this world, the loud music, the so-called pleasures that appear so attractive, few find fulfilment and substantial happiness from the world's aimless activities.

Instead of experiencing fullness of life, we have become an over-tense and highly-strung generation, suffering from devastating stress and strain. Tension and fatigue are the malady of our time.

Jesus warned, 'Whosoever shall drink of this water (worldly pursuits) shall thirst again.' God's word through Jeremiah was: 'My people have committed two evils; they have forsaken me the fountain of living waters, and hewed them out cisterns, broken cisterns, that can hold no water' (found false substitutes and pleasures that are useless).

When the explorer Counthart perished in the Australian desert, a note was found by his dead body inside his tent: 'Lost, lost for want of water.'

Many today have no water, no spiritual *life*. They feel frustrated, despised, forlorn, weary, worn and sad. A woman said to a minister I know, 'What do I want God for? I have three cars, a detached house, a country cottage, a microwave, four colour TVs, holidays abroad, videos, compact discs. I have everything.'

A week later, he had a phone call, and heard a weeping broken voice. It was this same woman, asking the minister to pray and to visit her. When he enquired what had changed her mind so quickly, she cried, 'My son tried to commit suicide today. . .'

All her possessions could not give her son life. He was tired of the legacy of empty materialism she had passed on.

None of the systems, human agencies and efforts of men can give Life!

No wonder Margaret Asquith wrote, 'A well written life is as rare as a well spent life.'

Let us stop and look at our lives. Am I getting out of it all that I could, or should? Am I missing something? How can I find life that's real, that counts, that's fulfilling and thrilling?

As we look at our lives we may discover how foolish we really are. What wrong emphasis we may have, what we are missing, what vital values we have failed to comprehend or have lost hold of. Tension, irritation at home, blowing up in the office or business, flying off the handle with the kiddies. What is this inner unrest? What is the answer?

We find an unease and dissatisfaction at the core of our being, a need, a hunger for something outside of the human will, for something hard to define but desperately wanted. We find deep inner fears a longing for the eternal, a kind of homesickness of the soul. Man has a hunger which earth cannot satisfy. He does not live by bread alone; he has immortal longings in him. Often people say, 'I want something, but I do not know what it is I want.' Nothing produced by this planet can meet the deep longings of our souls. As Augustine said to God: 'Thou hast created us for thyself.'

Life does not depend on *things*—a nice home, an adequate income, a wide circle of friends, or congenial work, or good health. The world says you can be happy if you have these things, that you are unhappy if you lack them. But the greatest blessing of all is denied by this world and its pleasures, possessions and pursuits: the blessing of inward rest!

Thoreau wrote, 'Most men live lives of quiet desperation,' and Tennyson echoed – 'O that the man I am might cease to be. . .'

Dante said, 'I am searching for that which every man seeks – peace and rest!'

At the end of his 'Question Time' programme on TV in Britain, Sir Robin Day says what is almost a mockery to millions: 'Sleep well'. Multitudes just cannot! For they are just unable to cope with a fearful, stressful, confusing and tension-filled world.

What is the answer? God wants you to live! Jesus said, 'I am come that they might have life and have it more abundantly'—to the fill, till it overflows!

'To be carnally minded is death,' Paul declared, 'to be spiritually minded is life and peace.'

God wants to give you more than the grey gaudiness, the artificial gaiety, the stress, the blustering rat-race of the world. He wants you to become the person he intended you to be. Your life takes on a new dimension as you look at your problems through God's point of view!

It was 13 months after my first appearance on the famed 'Mike Baker Show' on Radio Pacific, Auckland, New Zealand, that I drove with my crusade organiser in that country, the Rev. John Coleman, into the car park of the radio studios in downtown Auckland. Looking through the glass partitions upstairs in the modern building was Mike himself, laughing and waving. He recognised me in my all-English 'Sherlock Holmes' hat—a rare oddity 'down under'!

Up in the lift a well dressed healthy-looking man smiled at me. I thought, 'Have I seen that face before?' Later John Coleman reminded me. He was the studio producer who had been such a sceptic last year but came in after so many had been healed on the spot. He was so impressed by it all that he had got healed of a very painful complaint in his neck and spine.

He had had no trouble with it since, I was told later by Mike Baker. We sat in Mike's spacious but rather full and untidy office, with papers everywhere. A secretary popped in. 'The phones are ringing already,' she announced. 'It's going to be a busy morning.'

Mike introduced the phone-in session. 'Great to see you here again, Melvin.' I recalled his reserve, caution, even cynicism just over a year earlier when for the first time ever in the history of New Zealand media, I had been invited to pray for five, and later a sixth, sick incurable people selected by the station 'live' in their programme, in a 3-hour show. (My book *The Greatest Miracle of All* gives a full account.)

Now what smiles, what enthusiasm! He explained that when they checked on the different cases I had prayed for months after I had gone, on a follow-up programme, all those healed had been so positive in their new-found health. 'We have them all back on the programme today, to see what they are like!' Mike enthused. 'The last I heard,' he went on, 'they were full of life . . .' He was to use that phrase often during the next three hours. So many calls came jamming in, because of the miraculous healings on the previous programme and the excellent reports from those healed last time, that the producer asked if I could stay on the phone-in for four hours, which I gladly did. A further six new folk came onto the show on this second programme and as I prayed for them, one after another received healing.

Mike talked to four people who had been in the studio last year and had experienced a wonderful new life in the past year. Joy had come to their families, new-found health to their bodies, they could walk again, go out shopping, painful diseases had gone, they could work, help their children. Each one used phrases like 'I have an entirely different life now' . . . 'totally different since this experience'. . . 'I have begun to live again'!

It was marvellous to realise that not only in great public healing meetings, or in evangelism services, or in individual counselling groups, but even in a busy independent national radio network station, crammed with world-wide news of despair, riot, coups, take-overs, corruption, violence, war, disease, famine and trouble, people were receiving *life*. They were experiencing power. . .health. . .vitality . . .joy. . .peace. . . God was there in all the hurly-burly.

As I left the studio on a high note of victory, my mind went back to the cry of the man I had spoken to some months earlier. He had asked, 'How can it work for me? I know you have a marvellous quality of life but how could I maintain it? – how long does it last? – I would love to keep a life like this as long as I can!'

As we drove through the busy streets of the Auckland suburbs, I thought about the keys to receiving and maintaining life, vitality, victory, joy, peace, for all of a person's life. Many thoughts crowded my mind in the days that followed, and I noted down one after another what it is that hinders us, what we overlook, what gives us endless flow, what is the source, what do we need to watch for that could creep in and steal and rob us of a hard-sought-after joy? How can we defeat fatigue, achieve and maintain effectiveness in our daily walk? How can we keep a keen interest in living, enjoy a more satisfying life, a greater sense of well-being, which will counteract stress and tension?

But we *can* maintain our new found life to the brim! We can truly 'live again'.

But I have learnt one important lesson and have taught it world-wide: none of us are living as fully as we could live!

After all everyone wants life to the full. As I showed in my book *Radiant Christian Living*, they want to achieve, they want to live a happy and successful life. We meet life's casualties everywhere: life went well for them, they set out with such vigour, but their enthusiasm has gone, their joy dried up, their mind assailed by doubt, hesitation, tension, stress and spiritual depression. They have come to a full stop. The road to fulfillment and life has become blocked.

I want to help you to stay alive, to rekindle life if it is at a low ebb, to bring excitement, vision, vitality, energy, fullness of joy to your life. I want to show you how you can be buoyed up by the love of God, so you never lose in the great battles of life, how you can unlock your faith-power, wait on and know God, and walk in dynamic power. Jonathan Swift, author of the famous book *Gulliver's Travels*, once put it aptly: 'May you live all the days of your life.' That is my prayer, and my purpose in writing this book.

III: *Is permanent happiness possible?*

How wrong Voltaire was when he said, 'God is a comedian playing to an audience that's afraid to laugh.' God wants us to have fun! *Fun is healthy*.

Dr Fosdick is reported to have said: 'There is enough tragedy in the New Testament to make it the saddest book in the world, yet it is the most joyful. It is an account of men and women who triumphed over the forces of evil. Their joy knew no bounds. No earthly power could stop them singing their psalms and hymns and spiritual songs. After five terrible beatings and two horrible stonings, Christianity's most versatile Apostle shouted jubilantly from his prison cell, "Rejoice and again I say unto you rejoice." Nearly all the books in the New Testament end on a joyful note.'

The famous writer A. A. Milne took his son to a theatre to see Cecily Courtneidge in a pantomime. He laughed and enjoyed it so much, a box of chocolates was sent up to his box from behind stage, with a little note. It read 'For the little boy who is laughing so much'!

We need to have some fun, to learn to express joy, to enjoy life. When the prodigal came home they had a great feast, they enjoyed themselves. One translation has it, 'Then the party began. . .' As Gerald Coates put it, 'let us be eating, drinking, and partying till Jesus comes'.

Not, of course, in an ungodly, worldly sense, but rather in free, relaxed, joyous living that is healthy and blessed.

Martin Luther said, 'If you're not allowed to laugh in heaven, I don't want to go there.'

Few human activities are so enjoyable as laughter. When we laugh we feel good, our cares are momentarily lifted and a sense of well-being suffuses the system. For centuries it has been said that laughter is the best medicine, and now science is telling us why. Over the past few years researchers in France, America and Canada have been seriously investigating the health benefits of laughter, and have been studying what happens to people when they laugh.

According to one French doctor, Pierre Vachet, laughter can deepen breathing, expand blood vessels, improve circulation, speed tissue healing and stabilise many body functions. In short, it acts as a powerful drug. But, unlike many drugs chemically produced in the laboratory, laughter has no adverse side-effects.

Dr Paul Elkman writing in *Science* magazine says all his experiments show 'a smile controls the whole of the nervous system and many other vital functions. The human grin produces a powerful support to life and physical well-being, and is like an umbrella against life's storms.'

A lady's passport photo was so miserable that the officer at immigration control at a certain airport said to the tourist, 'If you look that bad, my dear, you *need* a holiday!'

The critics have unjustly attributed to Jesus the depression of the graveyard. Somehow they have missed the point that Jesus was 'anointed with the oil of gladness above his fellows'. Although he was 'acquainted with grief', the ministry of Christ was one of cheering the hearts of men. A large part of his classic Sermon on the Mount shows how men may come into the blessed state of happiness.

The Church seems to have forgotten that Christ was born in a burst of angelic joy. It is quite amazing how, over the centuries, there have been attempts to do away with this vital aspect of the Gospel. Years ago, sobersides in the Church would stop the singing, stifle the holy laughter, frown on humour, and remove the organ music, as it was thought to be carnality.

Many churchgoers still suspect that anything funny is subversive. They fail to catch the humorous overtones of Jesus when he used the illustration of a camel trying to squeeze through the eye of a needle, or the man trying to get a splinter out of someone else's eye when there was a plank in his own!

The great element of Christianity is joy. The Bible speaks of holy men dancing, leaping and shouting for joy. This experience is described by words pregnant with meaning, like 'great', 'abundant', 'exceeding' and 'unspeakable'.

Generally speaking, the Church has become so dignified today that should anyone enter a rapturous experience like the Apostles, who were intoxicated with the new wine of the Holy Spirit at Pentecost, they would not only be unwelcome to the ecclesiastical ranks but branded as fanatical heretics.

The happiness of which the Bible speaks is not, as some suppose, only of a heaven to be hoped for hereafter. This is not true to the facts of spiritual life. The man who has had an encounter with God and has submitted himself to him grasps eternity now. He experiences a foretaste of heaven on earth. His happiness is real, deep and abiding, even in the midst of persecution and adverse circumstances.

The Psalmist said confidently 'He will make me smile again. . .' (Psalm 43:5, Living Bible). Solomon said, 'A merry heart maketh a cheerful countenance' Proverbs 15:13).

Someone asked Rufus Moseley whether Jesus ever laughed, and he replied: 'I don't know, but he certainly fixed me up so I can!' As Tertullian put it so well: 'The Christian saint is hilarious.'

The early Christians possessed a radiancy even in the face of death. When they were thrown to the lions and burned at the stake, the blessed hope that welled up within their hearts was unquenchable. They possessed not only a message but an experience and they lived and died in a holy endeavour to raise the drooping spirits of those who were without God and without hope in the world.

How can we become like that? It is a question which surely deserves out closest study.

It is interesting to read what men of ancient times thought about it. Plato said, 'We must find happiness by taking an interest in the things of life. We must love life, but remember that after death we shall live again.'

St Augustine, the Christian Father, makes a most interesting observation here. 'Be not over-interested in this life; think with Plato, that it is only a state contrary to the original nature of man – but instead of seeking, like Zeno, a saviour in yourself, seek him in God alone, the wisdom which has become incarnate in Jesus Christ our Lord.'

Yet Augustine does not give the full answer here. Complete happiness comes to us when relationships with both God and man are on a correct basis. In the first place absolute submission to the Creator is necessary, which means obeying his Word and walking according to his laws; secondly, rendering unselfish service to others, helping the sad, the poor, the lonely and destitute – that is, loving one's neighbour as oneself.

One great man recommended it as a rule that we should try to make at least one person happy every day. He concluded that in ten years 'you will have made 3,650 persons happy or brightened a small town by your contribution to the fund of genuine joy.' We should all try to act upon this suggestion.

Learn to laugh at circumstances. You will not get through the many pressures that come against you without a sense of humour. The radiant man is not down for long, if he learns to laugh at his problems. Ella Wilcox, the great actress of the past, used to say, 'Laugh and the world laughs with you; weep and you weep alone.' Jesus was a man of laughter and joy. 'I have spoken unto you that my joy might remain in you, and that your joy might be full.' T.E.Brown said of Jesus, 'Methinks in Him there dwells always a sea of laughter very deep.' Paul said, 'The Kingdom of God is joy,' or, as it might be translated, 'happy faces from the heart.'

At the end of a large crusade meeting, I often retire to my digs or to our hotel or motel, or perhaps might be invited to the minister's manse. After a shower or bath,

I return to my team and we often sing and even dance around the room, often in endless infectious laughter, sometimes till we are hoarse! When we have seen the joy on so many faces, when miracles and healings have flowed and so many have been converted to Christ, knowing tremendous victories have been won for the Cross, we cannot keep from rejoicing in exuberant happiness. Jesus said, 'Let no man take this joy from you. . .'

It is possible to lose joy and laughter. To let materialism, over-emphasis on possessions, bitternesses, the rat-race of this world steal your joy. Jesus said you could be robbed of happiness. Look around you at the people in the office, factory, business house, in the shops and down your street – look at their faces. There is little contentment and even less laughter!

The story is told of a successful businessman, who bought his morning paper from the newspaper man at the station entrance on his way to the office each day. When the man sold him the paper, he always had some crude, melancholy statement to make, some pessimistic coarse comment. The businessman's companion commented, 'You are always cheerful with that fellow, saying nice things to him, when he is so rude. Why not buy your paper in the shop outside or speak to him sharply?' With a radiant, beaming face he said, 'Why should I let him dictate my attitude in life? Why should I let him spoil my joy?'

Ecclesiastes says, 'There is a time to laugh' (3:4). Thomas Hobbes the philosopher said, 'Laughter is nothing else than a sudden glory.'

It is vital to life. It is the spice of life. It is vital to health and wholesome living. The man or woman who overcomes and is a winner is the one who has found the secret to happiness. *It is one of God's great gifts.*

Solomon commented, 'A merry heart doeth good like a medicine' (Proverbs 17:22).

Dr Roy Hicks said, 'The laughing Christian is the victorious Christian, the joyful Christian is the one who always has the victory. . .'!

Here are the seven ways to permanent happiness and peace.

1. Have a right attitude of mind

Many have spoken about the importance of attitude. Solomon: 'As he thinketh (imagines) in his heart, so is he' (Proverbs 23:7).

The psalmist: 'We have thought of thy loving kindness' (Psalm 48:9).

Paul: 'Love. . .thinketh no evil' (1 Corinthians 13:5). 'Casting down imaginings, and every high thing that exalteth itself against the knowledge of God, and bringing into captivity every though to. . . Christ' (2 Corinthians 10:5).

Jesus: 'Thou shalt love the lord thy God. . .with all thy mind.' A mind purified, fortified by faith in Jesus, filled with his thoughs, is one full of joy.

Disraeli: 'Nurture great thoughts, for you will never go higher than your thoughts.'

Milton: 'The mind is its own place, and in itself can make a Heaven of Hell, or a Hell of Heav'n.'

Napoleon was a typical picture of this. He had riches, power, glory, popularity, yet he said on St Helena, 'I have never known six happy days in my life.' Yet blind, deaf, dumb Helen Keller could write, 'I have found life so beautiful'!

Captain Scott and his two companions died in the Antarctic snow 'singing ringing songs of cheer'. The words of Montaigne, the great French philosopher, were the motto of his life: 'A man is not hurt so much by what happens, as by his opinion of what happens.'

All that great men achieve is the result of winning the battle in their minds. A man can rise no further than his thoughts allow him.

Emerson wrote, 'A man is what he thinks about all day long. . .'

God has designed our beings in such a way that right attitudes in the mind produce right effects in the body. As William James put it: 'The greatest revolution in my generation was the discovery that human beings, by changing their inner attitudes of mind, could alter the outer aspects of their lives.'

Paul said that without the redemptive love of Christ 'we are of all men most miserable'. But discovering God's love, care and compassion, we are saved from misery. Life begins!

A little boy was moaning and fussing after his Mum had spent no end of money on him at a circus. Finally she gripped him by the collar and shook him still his teeth rattled. 'Now enjoy yourself. Do you hear? Have a good time, make sure you do, or I'll give you what for. . .'

People think happiness is having things, going places, receiving gifts, having pleasure, instead of seeing it is a state of heart and mind. It is what you have inside of you. As an old line goes: 'As man's created spirit up the ladder God-ward mounts, he finds it isn't altitude but attitude that counts.'

2. Happiness lies in a close relationship and abiding contact with Jesus.

Jesus gives us an abundant, overflowing joy. Kendell Harris says: 'Joy is the strength of the people of God; it is their glory, it is their characteristic mark. And when the mark is absent, then the characteristic of a Christian is absent.' Scripture says: 'We enjoy our redemption' (Ephesians 1:7, Moffatt). To be redeemed and not enjoy the redemption is a contradiction in terms: joy is inevitable in the heart of a truly redeemed Christian.

Drink deep of the life of Jesus, and you will know the experience of which Wesley wrote:

My God, I am thine, what a comfort divine,
What a blessing to know that my Jesus is mine,
In the heavenly Lamb, thrice happy I am
And my heart it doth dance at the sound of His name.

Dance? If you can't dance, then settle for throwing your hat in the air!

How often people have told me the same story in my many Crusades all over Britain and across the world. As one lady expressed it, 'I never associated religion or Christianity with happiness. Now I'm saved – I'm as happy as a lark!'

'The ransomed of the Lord will return. They will enter Zion with singing; everlasting joy will crown their heads. . .' (Isaiah 35:10, NIV).

A drama student, on seeing the face of a Christian doctor, said to a friend, 'I'd be a Christian if I could be as joyful as he is.' It says of Jesus in the New Testament, 'Though you do not see him now, you believe in him and are filled with an inexpressible and glorious joy' (1 Peter 1:8, NIV).

3. Happiness is ours when we count our blessings.

It is good to remember how blessed we are, how fortunate we are. We live in days of rampant hardness in which most folk take everything for granted.

A doctor said to a well-known writer, 'At the end of the day I am tired. Ah, but I'm a thankful man. I've dealt with a lot of patients since breakfast, all with something wrong, all suffering in some way, and here I am turned 60 years, fit and well, able to take two steps at a time. . . for every blessed hour of reasonable health and strength and sufficient energy can I do less than thank God!'

It is healthy to have a thankful heart. To remember what God has done for us, what life has given to us. Gipsy Smith said, 'Memory is the most blessed faculty given to man.'

Remember good things. W.Somerset Maugham, the great short-story writer, stayed in the most famous hotels in the world. Always, even when staying in the renowned Raffles Hotel in Singapore, he brought his own cup with him. It was a shabby looking and slightly cracked old cup and he used it at every meal.

When asked about it, he replied that when he drank he looked at that old cup and had thankful memories of how he started so poor and humble, but had been so blessed in life. He wanted always to be thankful!

Dr Mervyn Stockwood, the Anglican Bishop, used to say that when up against difficulties and problems he would think of three things for which he was dearly thankful for in life, and it eased the burden. . .

In H.G.Wells' book *The History of Mr Polly,* the whimsical little character, who never seems to get anything right, is a constant failure, and is nagged to death by his utterly frustrated wife, is invited on Sunday morning to go to church with her. They are in the midst of very hard times, and Mr Polly refuses, declaring, 'I've nothing to be grateful for.'

How different the person who suffers a great loss, yet is thankful for past blessings. It happened in Cumbria when a lovely Christian family had their beautiful view of the hills and lakes blocked by a new estate built right across their front windows. All they could see was bricks and mortar, road and cars. Asked why they did not protest they replied, 'We have had the benefit of this view for 25 years, now it's someone else's turn.' Thankfulness for the years of refreshing eye salve and breathtaking beauty, but no resentment at what they had lost.

Samuel Pepys records in his famous diary, written during the reign of Charles II, that when he became wealthy, he never lost what was really important. 'Mighty proud am I, and ought to be grateful to God Almighty that I am able to have a spare bed for my friends. . .' He generously gave accommodation and hospitality to many people, remembering what goodness had been showered upon him.

The giving of thanks is God's will! He loves a thankful people.

There is great happiness in counting your blessings. You may have heard the famous verse:

> I had the blues
> because I had no shoes,

> Until upon the street
> I met a man who had no feet.

Cromwell had a motto put up in his churches throughout England: 'Think and thank' – remember your blessings.

The philosopher Schopenhauer pointed out, 'We seldom think of what we have but always of what we lack.' Dr Samuel Johnson said, 'The habit of looking on the best side of every event is worth more than a thousand pounds.'

Solomon spoke of 'the memory of the just. . .' being so good. How true.

> Count your blessings,
> Name them one by one. . .
> Count your many blessings. . .
> There are millions more. . .

I used to sing those words as a lad in Sunday School, not realising how true they were till later in life.

4. To keep permanent happiness, never seek revenge or to get even.

Seeking revenge is a great destroyer of happiness. Believers must not act like the world, but turn the cheek as Jesus said.

As Shakespeare put it.

> Heat not a furnace for your foe so hot
> That doth singe yourself.

Seeking to hit back only weakens our hand. Churchill, when faced with the evil of Nazism, did not react as they expected but replied, 'what sort of people do they think we are?. . .'

We will not act in a way Jesus would not behave or in a way he would not expect of us.

Edith Cavell, the British heroine of the First World War, uttered these last words before being shot: 'I realise that patriotism in not enough. I must have no bitterness or hatred towards anyone.'

Or as General Eisenhower aptly expressed it, 'Let's not waste a moment thinking ill about anyone we don't like.'

Jonathan Edwards, the great revivalist, made a resolution in his early life, which he said was the source of his fruitful happy life. It was 'to resolve never to do anything which I should despise or think meanly of in another. To resolve never to do anything out of revenge.'

5. For true happiness, be yourself.

The old saying of English preachers was 'Play only one tune, and the best way to start is on B natural.' God uses men as they are. Look at Billy Bray, a real eccentric, dancing on his wife's grave, rejoicing because she had made it to Glory! He influences thousands even today.

W.P.Nicholson was a rough diamond if ever there was one. Blunt and crude, it was not unknown for him to come down from the pulpit and silence a heckler in a tough way. Yet he won multitudes to Christ and saved Ulster from civil war.

Look at George Jefferies, the gentleman preacher from South Wales with his quiet, powerful manner that raised up and inspired 300 churches in Britain in the 1920s and 1930s.

We must let God gift us and work through the channel we are.

Sir Walter Raleigh, professor of English literature at Oxford in 1904 (not the one who lost his head in the tower), said, 'I can't write a book commensurate with Shakespeare – but I can *write a book by me.*'

Be yourself. Act on the sage advice that Irving Berlin gave George Gershwin. When Berlin and Gershwin first met, Berlin was famous but Gershwin was a struggling young composer working for 35 dollars a week in Tin

Pan Alley. Berlin, impressed by Gershwin's ability, offered him a job as his musical secretary at almost three times the salary he was then getting. 'But don't take the job,' Berlin advised. 'If you do, you may develop into a second-rate Berlin. But if you insist on being yourself, some day you'll become a first-rate Gershwin.'

When Charlie Chaplin first started making films, the director insisted on Chaplin's imitating a popular German comedian of that day. Charlie Chaplin got nowhere until he acted himself.

Douglas Malloch wrote:

> If you can't be a pine on the top of the hill
> Be a scrub in the valley – but be
> The best little scrub by the side of the rill,
> Be a bush, if you can't be a tree.
>
> If you can't be a bush, be a bit of the grass
> And some highway happier make;
> If you can't be a muskie, then just be a bass
> But the liveliest bass in the lake!
>
> If you can't be a high tree then just be a trail,
> If you can't be the sun, be a star;
> It isn't by the size that you win or you fail,
> Be the best of whatever you are.

Evelyn Waugh summed it all up:

> I am not he,
> she is not he,
> and *they* are not ME'!

6. Learn from your trials – don't let them mar your happiness.

Some people just go flat as soon as things go wrong for them. The old verse says:

> I walked a mile with pleasure,
> She chatted all the way,
> But left me none the wiser,
> For all she had to say.
>
> I walked a mile with sorrow,
> And ne'er a word said she.
> But oh the things I learned from her,
> When sorrow walked with me!

Your life and your faith will not travel through a field of roses, but through much turbulence which will test and prove them. A small project tries you in a small way, a big project tries you in a big way. Get something out of the most trying times.

In Joseph Conrad's bestseller *Typhoon*, a seaman on a ship faces a terrific storm. Tossed to and fro, almost capsized, he tells the captain, 'Always face it, Captain Macquire, that's the way to get through the storm. . .'

The old verse tells us that God guides and takes care of us, but also that out of dangers and distressing occasions can come much good.

> Sometimes the lions' mouths are shut,
> Sometimes God bids us fight or fly;
> Sometimes he feeds us by the brook,
> Sometimes the flowing stream runs dry.
>
> The danger that his love allows
> Is safer than our fears may know;
> The peril that his care permits
> Is our defence where'er we go. . .

In C.S.Lewis's allegory *Pilgrim's Regress*, when he looks back over the ground seeing things afresh in the light given to him, at the end of his first journey, he records, 'It is good to reflect, how marvellous if we could take the journey of life with the hindsight or experience of having been over the ground before! But we cannot, we are only once in this life.'

We must learn from life's trials and turn them to good! May we say with Ezekiel, 'It is a trial. . . (but) it shall be no more' (Ezekiel 21:13)!

Paul and Peter testified to the value of learning from trials and turning them to our well-being. 'The trial of your faith, being much more precious than of gold . . . though it be tried . . . might be found unto praise and honour and glory' (I Peter 1:7). 'In a great trial of affliction. . . their joy. . . abounded' (2 Corinthians 8: 2–3).

Henry Ford said, 'If I can't handle a problem I let it handle itself.'

A lady said, 'I accept the inevitable.' When Thomas Carlyle heard that he snorted, 'By gad she'd better!' Yes, and you and I had better accept the inevitable, too! If we rail and kick against it and grow bitter, we won't change the inevitable; but we will change ourselves for the worse!

We can live in spite of trials or use them for good!

Walt Whitman wrote, 'Oh, to confront night, storms, hunger, ridicule, accident, rebuffs as the trees and animals do.'

The late Dean Hawkes of Columbia University declared that he had taken a Mother Goose rhyme as one of his mottoes:

> For every ailment under the sun,
> There is a remedy, or there is none;
> If there be one, try to find it;
> If there be none, never mind it.

Or in the words of the old boxing term: '*Roll with the punch*'!

On TV in Britain we have a cigar advertisement in which a man always gets in 'tight corners'. He loses a contract, his car slips off brake and runs away, his lady jilts him. Each time he settles down and forgets it all – when he smokes his Panatella! But a cigar is not a real comfort – we must rise above trials. Paul urged us, when faced with impossible situations to use the trials to let them shape us for good.

George V had these framed words hanging on the wall of his library in Buckingham Palace: 'Teach me neither to cry for the moon nor over split milk.' The same thought is expressed by Schopenhauer in this way: 'A good supply of resignation is of the first importance in providing for the journey of life.'

Once when Ole Bull, the world-famous violinist, was giving a concert in Paris, the A string on his violin suddenly snapped. But Ole Bull simply finished the melody on three strings. 'That is life,' comments Harry Fosdick, 'to have your A string snap and finish on three strings.'

That is not only life. It is more than life. It is life triumphant! Nietzche's formula for the superior man was not only to bear up under necessity but 'to love it'.

The more I study the careers of men of achievement, the more convinced I am that a surprisingly large number succeeded because they started out with handicaps that spurred them on to great endeavour and great rewards. As William James said, 'Our infirmities help us unexpectedly.'

It is highly probable that Milton wrote better poetry because he was blind, and that Beethoven composed better music because he was deaf.

Helen Keller's brilliant career was inspired and made possible because of her blindness and deafness.

If Tchaikovsky had not been frustrated and driven almost to suicide by his tragic marriage, if his own life had not been pathetic, he probably would never have been able to compose his immortal 'Symphonie Pathétique'.

If Dostoevsky and Tolstoy had not led tortured lives, they would probably never have been able to write their outstanding novels.

Paul said, 'Tribulation (rightly used of course) worketh patience, and. . . hope' (Romans 5:3–4).

William Bolover penned these words:

The most important thing in life is not to capitalise on your gains. Any fool can do that.

The really important thing is to profit from your losses. That requires intelligence; and it makes the difference between a man of sense and a fool.

7. Happiness never fades when we bring joy to others.

I remember the old fiery preacher Alistair Smith of the Salvation Army saying years ago when I was a boy, 'The more you give Jesus away, the more you'll have of *him*. . .and the more you'll have of *real life*!'

How true! The key is to give of yourself. In the words of the motto of the Prince of Wales, 'Ich dien' – I serve.

Or as Benjamin Franklin put it, 'When you are best to others you are best to yourself.' The Chinese in Malaysia told me their old saying: 'A bit of fragrance clings to the hand that gives the roses.'

Dreiser advocated: 'I shall pass this way but once. Therefore any good that I can do or any kindness that I can show – let me do it now. Let me not defer nor neglect it, for I shall not pass this way again.'

The Bible teaches: 'Give and it shall be given unto you'

Jesus taught, 'It is more blessed – it is happier—to give than to receive.'

Mattern said: 'The way to happiness. . .keep your heart free from hate, your mind from worry, live simply, give much, fill your life with love, scatter sunshine, forget self, think of others. . .'

IV: *How to have a nervous breakdown*

How can you bring on nervous exhaustion, anxiety neurosis, mental fatigue and collapse or a full breakdown? Follow any or all of these five steps.

(In case you prefer *not* to live a nervously distressed life, I'll tell you later how to prevent it.)

1. Think only of yourself.

Act like a spoilt child and try to get your own way in everything. Sulk every time you don't get what you want, and expect a pat on the back each time you do something worthwhile. This is good for arousing people's antagonism towards you. It's the way to terminate friendships.

Then remember, the road to confusion and increase in tension is to be introspective. Believe and harbour every thought that comes into your mind about yourself, without discrimination.

How powerful the human mind is. If we allow them, thoughts will produce a persecution complex. Many unfortunate folk are in mental homes today because of this.

Some have a disease complex. Doctors will tell you that one of the worst things that can happen to anybody is to allow the mind to dwell on aches, pains and symptoms of the body. This is one proven way to create nervous tension and bring on sickness of various kinds.

I know one lady who for years seemed to delight in indulging in long moody sessions of self-pity, counting her heartbeats and waiting for palpitations to develop. No specialist could convince her that there was nothing wrong with her. When her relations realised what was happening they refused to pamper her any longer. She got better speedily.

Someone has said that 'selfishness is the seed of the evil spirit'. All that is necessary to bring big trouble into your life is to cultivate this seed.

2. Try to re-live the past.

Join the thousands of people who are trying to do what is literally impossible, to bring back the irrevocable. What has been done cannot be undone, whether it be good or bad. The past is the region of fact, pleasant or painful. It is, generally speaking, as we have made it, and over it the imagination has no power. Yet many today are 'living on their nerves' as a result of trying to think their way out of this impasse.

Be sure to ignore the advice of the apostle Paul, who said, 'Forgetting those things which are behind.' Take no notice of the scriptural exhortation to ask God's forgiveness for any past misdemeanours.

To some people, of course, the past has not been one of failure and mistakes, but glorious achievement. However, these also often get into a state of melancholy because they dwell on their successes and achievements and then moan over the fact that they are no longer riding the crest of the wave. They adopt the attitude that life could never be as interesting and as significant as in bygone days. To get into this situation, become a confirmed pessimist. Defeatism has all the ingredients to form a super cloud of gloom over your life.

3. Tax yourself to the limit.

Here is a great idea for those who are bent upon being a nervous wreck. Try to be a superman. Constantly carry a double load, don't take time off. Work seven days a week and twenty-four hours a day if possible. It will speed things up a bit if you follow the example of some people I know and have two or three jobs at a time.

As for holidays, simply adopt the attitude that they are a waste of time and that the suggestion to 'come apart and rest awhile' is only for folk bordering on infirmity. Refuse to heed the warnings of medical doctors that the body needs rest and relaxation. Then you have every chance of not living to become one of the 'old fogies'.

Long ago John Bate wrote a sensible bit of advice that we should all note. He said, 'As in pieces of machinery, whether a watch in the pocket or a locomotive on the railway, if it be driven beyond the power bestowed upon it by the maker it will break in some of its parts, and, for a time at least, be rendered useless; so with man, if his body or mind be taxed with work, whether in quantity or quality, beyond its capabilities, it will soon give way under the pressure, and require a respite for its restoration.'

4. Carry tomorrow's burdens.

This is one of the best ways to live in misery. An effective plan to adopt to stop yourself from enjoying life at the present time is to anticipate the troubles of years ahead. Add yesterday's and tomorrow's burdens to today's and you will soon worry yourself into a fine old state of mental sickness.

On this subject men make the mistake of supposing that to look forward into the future means we must look anxiously forward. But surely we may just as easily look forward with hope as with despair. The Bible doesn't tell us to neglect planning for the future, but urges us not to do it with anxious fear.

With regard to our everyday problems, Jesus told us to live a day at a time. He said, 'Don't worry at all about tomorrow, tomorrow can take care of itself ! One day's trouble is enough for one day' Matthew 6: 34 (Phillips). But, of course, you must not take any notice of such sound advice.

5. Turn your back upon problems.

Another step towards a breakdown is to stubbornly refuse to be a realist and face up to complex situations. Believe that by ignoring problems they will somehow resolve themselves. Live in a dream world of unreality and never take positive steps to correct any blunders or repair any breaches. If you do decide to attempt to deal with any crisis or dilemma, then be sure to tackle the situation in your own strength, relying on your own wits to see you through.

As for the scriptural exhortations to 'Cast your burden on the Lord' and 'If any man lack wisdom let him ask of God who giveth to all men liberally', treat that as religious sentimentalism.

These five suggestions, if acted upon, will result in vexation of the spirit and a sense of frustration, leading to a serious setback in health, both of mind and body, with the guarantee that the way back to restored health will be a long uphill climb.

Carl Jung said that during 35 years as a psychiatrist, every one of his patients over the age of 35 had fallen ill because he or she had lost what living religion had given them, and none had been healed who did not regain his religious outlook.

Augustine declared 'Thou hast created us for thyself, and our heart cannot be quieted till it find repose in thee.' The demands of our turbulent natures are not calmed by human will alone; we need much more.

'I sought the Lord, and he heard me, and delivered me from all my fears.' Living in a world that is rife with fears, this statement is particularly appropriate and one that we should consider carefully.

There are said to be 24 basic phobias which are broken down into 650 secret fears that affect men and women. These are splintered into thousands of fiendish images in the minds of people who are scared.

It is surprising how many famous men, who were not at all worried about the things that upset most people, were terrified at the sight of insignificant creatures. Like Hitler, who became hysterical when a spider got near him. I have known people so fearful that they were unable to cross over a bridge or go outside the town in which they lived.

There is, of course, the healthy kind of fear which is inbred in all of us and for which we should be grateful, like being afraid to go near the edge of a cliff in case we fall over, or to swim out too far when we are in the sea for fear of being swept away. Then it serves to protect us. Fear is a wonderful servant, but a terrible master. One great man explained it in his way: 'Fear sometimes adds wings to the heels, but sometimes nails them to the ground and fetters them from moving.'

Some unhealthy fears that have possessed men through the ages, such as economic insecurity, old age and loneliness, are a very real factor today for many people.

Perhaps one of the most common fears today is to imagine one has a malignant disease. Only God knows how many people torture themselves because they are afraid they have cancer.

One lady I know just would not accept the fact that her fear was groundless, even after being told by a specialist, who had given her a thorough examination, that she was free from cancer. When the thought becomes deeply embedded in the mind like this, it is very serious. Different doctors reported her fit, but she refused to believe, and finally this fear brought on a real cancer from which she died. Fear killed her.

It is a well-known fact that when the mind becomes obsessed with thoughts of some dread disease, the symptoms and pains have followed, even though the sickness is not present.

A minister friend of mine had terrible stomach pains for almost two years. Often he was doubled up in agony. He went to many doctors, but they could find nothing wrong with him. Ultimately he made an appointment to visit a distinguished specialist. My friend was thoroughly examined. Then the specialist talked to him and confirmed what the other doctors had said previously, that there was not the slightest thing wrong with him. Then, when he was about to leave, the specialist said, 'When you go through that door, the pain will leave you. Just believe that.' It happened exactly as predicted, and that minister has been free from pain from that day to this.

Another fear is so foolish, and yet, I would venture to suggest, common to most people to some degree. It is the fear of what people think of them.

This can be a good thing, of course. In some ways it is right to be concerned about people's opinions. It can serve as a challenge and stimulates us to live as we ought.

Paul exhorts Christians to so arrange their lives as to 'provide things honest in the sight of all men', or, as Phillips translates it, 'See that your public behaviour is above criticism.' But there is a difference between trying to be an example before men and being in bondage to men.

Once we let this get out of hand we may get obsessed with the notion that folk are against us and become too scared to do anything in case they will not like it. This is an intolerable situation – a fearful prison of our own making.

Then again, fear of the past or the future affects many folk. Many a person has lived in terror because of some wrong they have committed in the past. They are afraid that they will be found out.

Even more, probably, are unnerved as they gaze into the future. Afraid that they will lose their friends and relatives and become infirm, afflicted and abandoned, they cannot enjoy the present because their thoughts are upon the unknown future. What a tyrant fear becomes when it gets out of hand!

Perhaps the greatest fear of all is that of death. The world calls this the 'king of terrors'. The thought of it certainly terrifies many. Alfred Krupp, the famous German manufacturer, was so gripped by this fear that he forbade his workers to ever mention the word death, and it is reported that he fled from his own home when a friend of his wife died. When his wife remonstrated with him about it, he left her. The result was a lifelong separation. It is claimed that when he came to die he offered his doctor a million dollars if he could prolong his life by ten years. But his money could not put off the appointment.

How wonderful then is the Psalmist's testimony, that he was delivered from all his fears. How can we too be free?

One way is to abandon ourselves to the will of God. Christ is a perfect example of this. In submitting to the Father, he found perfect freedom. He experienced the many vicissitudes of life, but was not alarmed by evil fears. How encouraging it must have been to his disciples to hear him say over and over again, 'It is I, be not afraid.' Resignation to the will of God abandons fears.

Complete trust in him can banish anxiety from our life also. I read recently of an aged Korean woman who was asked what benefit she had received from embracing the Christian faith. 'Many,' she replied. 'I will tell you of one, though you may not think it as important as I do. Before I was a Christian I never slept through the night without starting up and lying awake, sweating for fear lest the evil spirits were bringing some disaster on my family and property. Now when the sun sets, I commit family and possessions all to God, lie down, and sleep clear through till morning.'

Yes, we can find deliverance from all that would alarm us in a world of tumult, when it seems that civilisation is being shaken as by some demonic cataclysmic force bent on destruction. We may testify as David did, 'Though an host should encamp against me, my heart shall not fear; though wars should rise up against me, in this will I be confident,' because our trust is in the pillars of God's justice, mercy, truth and love which cannot fail.

Now the antidote to a nervous breakdown
1. Know a Personal God

Tennyson pondered:

> Flower in the crannied wall,
> I pluck you out of the crannies,
> I hold you here, root and all, in my hand,
> Little flower – but if I could understand
> What you are, root and all, and all in all,
> I should know what God and man is.

But we *can* know him.

The poet asked, 'In teeming millions can he care, can special love be everywhere?' The idea seems ludicrous to modern man. But Jesus said, the very hairs of your head are all numbered . . . You are of more value than many sparrows. Earthquake, trouble, cancer, famine, floods – all the ugly things of this world will be explained.

Those who have his peace 'shine forth as the sun . . .' Multitudes starve, multitudes are homeless, violence is rampant, but wherever there is God's peace there is radiance.

Marie Louise once wrote a letter to her husband Napoleon. Here was a man who shook the continent of Europe. He was in the midst of the battles of a lifetime, making history. And she wrote to him about simple things – mostly about their son's toothache! He had been in bed, he was getting up again soon – what a letter to a man engaged in world conquest! But does a general cease to be a father, an emperor cease to love and care about the small details of his son?

God is busy with world matters, taking care of millions, directing the Universe. Yet he is interested in you and me.

This personal God treats each one of us as an individual. Muller never asked for a penny, but prayed millions of pounds in. William and Catherine Booth could hardly pay the rent but raised an army of a million souls rescued from hell, and begged for money to feed millions of poor folk. God was with them both! Sadhu Singh crossed oceans without a dime to his name and played with leopards as if they were cats and his prayer life was impeccable. He did not feed the orphans like Muller, or win masses of unsaved like the Booths – but he did his own work as God gifted him!

To think we can all do the same and act the same is ridiculous! But we can all know him and obey him.

Of Paul's 13 letters preserved for us, many are short, barely half a page. But in them he says one thing over and over and over again: 'In Christ, in Christ.' The eminent German theologian Dr A. Deismann counted the number of times Paul used the words 'In Christ'. He found 164. It is the key to the very important secret of the bountiful life.

If any man be *in Christ*, he is a new creature.
I live, yet not I, but *Christ Lives in me*.

William Law, the great sage of the eighteenth century, wrote: 'A Christ not in us is a Christ not ours . . .'

We need Christ in us, living at the centre of our being, thinking, feeling and willing within our hearts. This is one of the timeless secrets of a boundless, bountiful life!

There *is* a personal God, and we can know him – personally.

2. Begin to enjoy and love simple things again.

L.S. Lowry was one of England's greatest modern painters. A lady protégé of Lowry was converted in one of my meetings in Cheshire. She told me about him. Instead of seeing the ugliness of the Lancashire mill towns, the darkness, the appalling semi–slavery, the dull, glum, hard life, he saw beauty in ordinary people. He saw through the 'dark Satanic mills'. That's why he painted his matchstick figures in white, with white backgrounds, white roads, whitish coloured sky and pavements, quite unlike the coal-blackened, smokey, wet, foggy, dismal pictures usually made of the old mill towns. He saw loveliness in the dark. He saw human people, families, homes, hearts, love, *life* in the dark!

Diana Rigg the actress was asked in an interview about the disasters in her life. How long did they last, and did she carry bitterness? 'Oh, they lasted till I got back home, then a disaster doesn't matter anymore . . .' She turned trials into nothing by love of home – love of the simple!

As Danny Kaye said shortly before he died, 'There is a child in every one of us . . .' See hope in a dark world. In all your difficult situations, keep simple, have hope, look with the eyes of a child, see only good in all things.

'The Lord preserveth the simple' sang the Psalmist. God's word 'giveth understanding to the simple . . . making wise the simple.'

'I Love Life' is the title of this fine poem by J.M. Robertson of Edinburgh:

I love life; I love each day,
I love when sunlight starts to stray
Through swaying trees, then pirouettes
Enhancing dancing silhouettes.

I love life; I love the sound
Of feathered friends, who gather round,
And with each magic melody
Provide a serenade that's free.

I love life; I love the sight
Of cloud-drifts on a moonlit night.
I love the lap of sea on shore
And every positive encore.

I love life; I love the kind
Of pleasures that invade the mind
Of faces, places, moments rare,
So fine and beautiful to share.

I love many other things
The privilege of living brings.

Despite the trouble and the strife,
So much to cherish . . . I love life.

3. Victory through song

In the economy of God song plays an important part. In the Old Testament Jehoshaphat's choir led the way to victory with song . . . and the enemy was scattered. In the New Testament Church, God saw the importance of keeping his troops triumphant, and commanded, 'When ye come together, every one of you has a psalm . . .' He encouraged them to win through song.

Indisputable miracles have been experienced and seen in my meetings as the marvellous atmosphere of God sweeps the congregation in song. People tell me everywhere that they were born again or they were healed during the singing in our meetings. It generates power.

James said, 'Is any (one) merry? Let him sing.'

Campbell Morgan warned, 'The Church has lost its first love when there is no song . . .'

Paul urged that we should be 'singing and making melody in your heart to the Lord'.

When the famous Whitefield's Tabernacle was destroyed in the bombing in 1944, in the damaged organ loft some sheets of old notepaper were found. They went back nearly 200 years. They read: 'make a large place for music in your life, it will bring you a priceless reward . . . In the hour of rest, music will lift your spirit, and give refreshment to every faculty . . . you will rejoice in the strength and energy which music will give . . . In the hour of prayer, music will quicken the aspirations of your soul . . . In the hour of fellowship, music will blend your spirit with others . . . in understanding . . .'

Song inspires, heals, brings a sense of God, uplifts, helps us defeat the stresses and tensions we face daily. The composer Franz Joseph Haydn wrote, 'When I think of God, my heart is so full that the notes leap and dance as they leave my pen . . .'

Christina Rosetti called heaven 'the homeland of music', for when our hearts are fixed on the Lord, they will sing whatever our personal feelings and circumstances.

A Lutheran bishop who was imprisoned in a Nazi concentration camp during the Second World War was one day singing a doxology. The SS officer beat him severely but could not silence him. The officer shouted, 'Don't you know I could shoot you now?' The bishop replied, 'Yes, I know. Do what you want, I have already died.' He then went on quietly singing. Thus Christians down through the ages have been able to quietly praise their God in music and song in the midst of the deepest afflictions.

There is happiness, relaxation, comfort in song. Madame Guyon spent years incarcerated in the Bastille in Paris. She faced great trials and tribulations, yet her writings are filled with joy and she has a continuous song. This fortress that caused some of the toughest men to go mad in its utter isolation became her heaven. She wrote, 'I am like a canary, which having lost its freedom can sing . . .' All contact with the outside world was severed for many long years, yet she sang:

> Strong are the walls around me,
> that hold me all the day,
> but they who thus have bound me,
> cannot keep God away;
> my very dungeon's walls are dear,
> because the God I love is here.

On one occasion a monastery was overrun by Norse invaders, and the monks were killed one by one. As in most medieval monasteries of that time, it was the custom that if one monk stopped singing, another would take over, so that day and night the building was filled with song and praise to God. As they were murdered one after another that day, the song finally ceased. Only one monk had been able to escape, and he hid in an inaccessible place. But when he heard the whole monastery fall silent, he instinctively took up the theme, and thus betrayed his hiding place. They soon found his whereabouts and took his life. Song should never cease, for it is this that constantly betrays the fact that we are the Lord's victorious people.

The magnificence of song touches even heaven itself. In Revelation 5:12 we read one of the great songs of heaven: 'Worthy is the Lamb . . .'

When Charles Wesley was still a very young Christian he was speaking to the godly Moravian evangelist Peter Bohler. Wesley was touched by Bohler's words: 'If I had a thousand tongues, I would praise Christ with all of them . . .' That statement so caught Charles' imagination that as he approached the first anniversary of his conversion, in thankfulness to the Lord he wrote, 'Oh, for a thousand tongues to sing my great Redeemer's praise . . .'

Dr Albert Schweitzer was rehearsing a Bach prelude on the organ in Ulm Cathedral. He asked a friend to stand at the back and let him know how it sounded. The friend said, 'You know I am no musician, I can't play a note . . .' Schweitzer replied, 'You are the one I want, to see how the "ordinary" person reacts.' In 20 minutes his friend was enraptured by the music, and Dr Schweitzer commented later, 'songs touch and inspire, even the ordinary.'

The sound of spiritual song especially has an 'atmosphere' that is out of this world. It gives something to us, it releases us from inhibitions, fears, nasty memories, tedium, and so on.

The old Romany Gipsies, when one of their number was depressed or broken down, danced around him or her, with simple heart-touching songs of joy, playing their violins. Soon the sad one was happy, cares all dispelled.

As we participate in 'singing unto the Lord' the morbid hindrances of life vanish.

Mary Slessor said, 'When I sing the doxology, I dismiss my doubts,' and that other great missionary, Amy Carmichael, said, 'When I sing in prayer the evil slips out of the room.'

King Saul found that when David sang, his anger, fears, nervous exhaustion, frustrations, began to evaporate. St Francis of Assisi was called 'God's minstrel'; his playing and singing brought so much healing, uplifting and joy.

How different from the emptiness of a song without a purpose, as in the fatalistic thinking of Thomas Hardy who wrote, 'Sing, it doesn't matter what you sing, as long as you sing!'

Spiritual song also helps us to move into true worship. Of course singing is not necessarily worship, but you cannot have much worship without song. Tozer said worship was song in which we 'feel Jesus in the heart'.

Graham Kendrick said, 'When all the external nature of things is removed and the inner something of the heart is made bare . . . and with true quality and quantity of our love and devotion we turn it to the King, then we are worshipping with a true song . . . Much modern worship is built around the absence of God, rather than his presence.' Thus in song from the depths of our beings, we touch a present Lord, rather than cry for an absent God.

Song in true worship brings in an indescribable atmosphere and presence of God in my meetings nationwide. So many have felt that 'touch' in the singing. People tell me on buses, on trains, in restaurants, in the streets, in hotels, in churches world-wide, how they were miraculously healed, how they were restored to faith in Christ, how they were revived and rejuvenated, rehabilitated, revitalised, remade, reborn by the Spirit of God—during the singing in one of these great Revival meetings.

If you are down . . . SING.
If you are overcome almost . . . SING.
If you are invaded with doubts . . . SING.
If you are alone . . . SING.
If you have had times that are hard . . . SING.
If you see no other way out . . . SING.

44

The famous writer J.B. Priestley told how in 1916 he watched line after line of British 'Tommies' marching along toward the Front, to the trenches of the Somme. They knew they were going to almost certain death, that few would survive, yet with a smile on their faces these young men, some looking like boys, marched along with stirring *singing*, their heads held high. It was a moving, inspiring sight which he never forgot.

Singing is mentioned nearly 200 times in the Bible. Many great men led the people of God forward in song and saw its inestimable value to lift the mind, heart and whole being. In Exodus Moses sang with the people, 'I will sing unto the Lord, for he hath triumphed gloriously.' Ezra had 200 singers (Ezra 2: 65). Singing is part of worship: 'All the earth shall worship thee, and sing' (Psalm 66: 4). It is pleasing: 'Sing praises unto his name; for it is pleasant' (Psalm 135: 3). It cleanses: 'In the transgression of an evil man there is a snare; but the righteous doth sing and rejoice' (Proverbs 29:6).

His business a failure, wandering the streets, dejected and near to suicide, J.C. Penney walked into a down-town mission. They were singing with fervour, these poor, cold street people: 'At the Cross, at the Cross where I first saw the light, and the burden of my heart rolled away . . .!' He saw their shining faces, the hope the words gave them, the vigour and lilt in their voices, and thought, 'If they have found hope through singing this old message, so can I.' So he did. Within an hour he walked out a changed man. He started again, and of course his great shops and stores today straddle the whole of the USA. And it all began with a song in that down-town mission hall!

No wonder in their enthusiasm Jezrahiah and his singers 'sang loud . . .' (Nehemiah 12: 42).

In the New Testament Church this power of song continued. Paul speaks of 'singing with grace in your hearts to the Lord' (Colossians 3: 16). James asked, 'Is any merry? Let him sing psalms.' The great apostle sang in 'the spirit and with the understanding' in tongues by divine gift, and with set songs and melodies. How often

45

in my meetings as hundreds have sung a new song in the Spirit, even the pianist borne along playing tunes he had not previously known, people have found relief of consciences, peace of heart, tensions flow, problems vanquished, deeper problems are met . . . *by divine song*!

Robert Louis Stevenson is remembered for his books and other writings. In his diary he once wrote: 'I have been to church today, am not depressed.'

We should go to worship joyfully expecting our God to speak through song to us!

No wonder David vowed, 'I will SING UNTO THE LORD AS LONG AS I LIVE' (Psalm 104: 33). He had experienced its uplifting therapy, sweet anointing, abundant energy, worthwhile value. With miracles innumerable, no wonder he wanted to sing!

3. Live hour by hour

From a forgotten author I culled this story: 'A pendulum had ticked the minutes by for 50 years in a respectable old clock in a farmer's kitchen. But one morning before the family was astir, to the amazement of all the other parts of the useful time-teller, it stood still. The old clock was just upon the point of striking, when all came to a sudden standstill. 'The truth is,' said the pendulum, 'I'm tired of this ticking.'

The dial-plate was enraged and said, 'You ought to be ashamed of yourself, you lazy wire.'

That stung the pendulum. 'Lazy wire indeed! And from you that have had nothing to do all the days of your life but to stare people in the face, while I have been at work every minute, shut up in this dark corner. Think of all I go through in 24 hours!'

The minute hand was quick at figures, and said, 'Yes, 86,400 times!'

'Exactly so,' said the pendulum. 'But I'm tired of it; so, think I to myself, I'll stop.'

But all the parts of the clock began to remonstrate with the revolutionary pendulum; and especially the dial which said, 'But recollect, that although you may think of a million strokes in an instant, you are only to execute one at a time, and you always have a moment given to you to swing in.' And then the weights, who had never been accused of light conduct, used their influence and implored the pendulum to go on.

So he took the advice and began to swing again and to tick as loudly as ever, and all the works proceeded in their accustomed way. Although, when the farmer came down to breakfast in the morning, he did wonder that his watch had gained so much time during the night.

The purpose of life is fulfilled by remembering that every minute's work has a minute in which to do it. Live an hour at a time, 24 hours a day.

God promised, 'As thy days, so shall thy strength be' (Deuteronomy 33: 25).

'The inward man is renewed day by day' (2 Corinthians 4: 16).

Solomon next – 'In the day of prosperity be joyful but in the day of adversity consider: God also hath set the one over against the other' (Ecclesiastes 7: 14).

Live an hour at a time – a day at a time. As the days pass, we may shut the door on them. They are over. We are travelling towards light and liberty, not towards darkness and fear. Tomorrow is a new day with a strength of its own. It is a good idea, often recommended, that each day we should tear off the page of the calendar that marks the day that is gone and mentally put that day away. Nothing can be altered. If it has been a good day, thank God. If a bad day, rejoice that it is over and you are neither in gaol nor in hospital! Tomorrow is another day. 'As thy days, so shall thy strength be.'

4. Ask God to help you daily.

As the old hymn says:

Thy secret tell; help me to bear
the strain of toil, the fret of care . . .

A lady picked up a simple phrase from the minister's sermon. After years of bitterness, hatred, fear, dissatisfaction, she wrote, 'Since I heard him say "EVERY DAY IS A GOOD DAY IF YOU PRAY", every night I list the things, I must be thankful for, little things that happened in the day. This habit has geared my mind to pick out the things that are nice, and forget the unpleasant. I have not had a single bad day for six weeks. I refuse to get downhearted. It is marvellous!'

LIVE DAILY! Do not frighten yourself into stress and worry by thinking of tomorrow. Thomas Carlyle used to say, 'Our main business is not to see what lies dimly at a distance, but to do what lies clearly at hand.' When Foreign Secretary during the First World War Viscount Grey wrote, 'If we look forward to the months and years ahead it would be very dreary and depressing, but we do not live in a lump, but day by day, and each day brings its own work and some expedient to help us . . .'
The poet wrote:

Every day is a fresh beginning;
Listen, my soul, to the glad refrain,
And, spite of old sorrow and older sinning
And puzzles forecasted, and possible pain,
Take heart with the day and begin again.

After all, did not Jesus teach us to pray, 'Give us this day our daily bread'? And day by day he will give us all the other things that we need. How futile it is to try today to carry tomorrow's burden! With the burden will come the strength and the guidance. Wasn't this what Jesus meant when he said, 'Don't fret about tomorrow. Today's cares are quite enough for today'?

It's equally important that we do not 'care' about yesterday. Let your yesterdays be gone forever. 'Forgetting those things which are behind . . . I press toward the MARK for THE PRIZE OF THE HIGH CALLING of God in CHRIST JESUS' (Philippians 3: 13,14).

Ask God to help you forget the haunting memories of yesterday, the failures of yesterday, the problems of yesterday, the bitterness, the difficult people, the unprincipled competitors in business, the losses you made. *Forget yesterday*! In the words of the anonymous author:

> I shut the door on yesterday
> And threw the key away,
> Tomorrow has no fears for me
> Since I have found today.

Dr Martin Luther King said, 'Let the dark yesterdays give way to a bright new tomorrow.'

Say with the famous writer Robert Browning, 'Our times are in his hands.' Put your life into God's hands, commit everything to him. Let God's hand be on your life, and under his direction you will grow, be blessed, move in joy and power and prosper on the right hand and on the left. In the words of the old verse:

> Moment by moment
> I'm kept by His love,
> Moment by moment I've life from
> above.

Live like this and you will overcome – you will avoid all excessive mental stress and breakdown.

V: *Triumphant prayer that always gets results*

A little girl asked her Daddy, a spiritually-cold Christian, a question one day with a mystified look on her face and a frown: 'Daddy, is God dead?'

Surprised by such a tiny one's query he replied, 'What do you mean, my dear?'

'Well, I used to hear you talking to him, but I never do now . . .'

What a rebuke. She had missed her father's prayers! Many today too have lost the art of true prayer.

Dr Paul Yonggi Cho from Korea, the minister of the largest church in the history of Christianity, wrote of this incredibly vital subject: 'I am asked is it possible for other nations of the world to have this kind of Revival we are experiencing . . . I am convinced that it is possible, if people dedicate themselves to pray . . . Why do we have this spiritual atmosphere, in which people are converted continuously in our meetings and in our church? The answer is prayer . . . God has no special children, we can all have power in prayer, if we are willing to pay the price . . . We must become familiar with prayer . . . In the morning hours of prayer I can feel His refreshing influence come over my heart, and I have the strength to go through the challenges of the day . . . prayer makes the difference . . . The letter killeth but the Spirit giveth life.'

We must learn to picket the Throne of Grace with perpetual prayer that brings a torrent of divine power unmatched on earth. This praying *always gets results*. It stirs God to act for us, it stirs God to move. The devil has set many traps to ensnare the Church into neglecting prayer, and he has become very successful at it. Our powers are dissipated.

Nehemiah knew the power of prayer when he came before the king to ask an impossible request. He began wisely, 'O King, I hope you live forever . . .' The king said, 'What do you want?' Nehemiah records, 'So I prayed to the God of heaven. And I said to the king . . .' He got his request and the people of God were on their way to restoring their nation and God's honour.

What is the praying that brings in reviving grace? It's prayer like that in west Wales in the past year or two, which has led to such a revival of power, conversions, miracles. One elderly lady who is almost 100 years old told me it was the greatest visitation in her district since Evan Roberts preached in the great Welsh Revival when she was a young girl.

A little church that prayed regularly once a month, all night, invited me for a mission. I was reluctant to accept first of all, but they prayed all the more and sought my answer, their elders coming 100 miles to my home to see me personally. I accepted, they prayed most earnestly, and God visited with hundreds of souls. This spread into Llanelli and other areas, one fellowship alone received 18 families to their church regularly, the Revival spread . . . *Prayer* – the only way!

> Prayer . . .
> obliterates immorality
> roots out heresy
> sweeps away jealousies.

Charles Finney wrote, 'Unless I experience prayer, I can do nothing . . . If for an hour I lose the spirit of grace and supplication, I am unable to preach with power and efficiency.'

Dr Skevington Wood in his lectures on the history of Revival said that they were always preceded and borne along by an 'absorbing concentration on prayer'. It was recorded of the Puritans of the sixteenth century, 'they do meet in holy prayer four times a day.' Four prayer meetings every day was their diet – no wonder they took over England!

The 'Holy Club' of Oxford was known for its pious sessions of prayer; this surely predestined the great evangelical awakening of the seventeenth century. John Wesley wrote, 'God does . . . everything by it,' and later added, 'I love prayer meetings, I know nothing where such a work of grace is wrought but here.'

He knew the truth of Jesus' words: Ask, and it shall be given you; seek, and ye shall find; knock, and it shall be opened unto you' (Matthew 7:7).

Thomas à Kempis said on one occasion, 'It is a great art to commune with God,' but few of us, it seems, have learned and applied the principles of effective prayer.

Yet all the children of God have an open invitation to the throne of grace. Not only do we have the privilege of 'waiting' in his presence and worshipping the Lord, but we can ask for needs to be met (Philippians 4:19), desires to be granted (Psalm 37:4), and the purposes of God to be worked out in our lives (Ephesians 1:11).

Real praying is expressed in those terms Jesus used, ask, seek and knock – words of inimitable simplicity, but of the utmost importance.

What an encouragement this promise is for all God's people who are feeling downhearted and frustrated. The Almighty can make the valley of Achar to become a door of hope, the wilderness a pool, and the desert to blossom as the rose! Nothing is too hard for the Lord and the invitation is extended to all to come to the One who can do the impossible and ask for deliverance. He is ready to give 'beauty for ashes, the oil of joy for mourning, the garment of praise for the spirit of heaviness' (Isaiah 61:3).

And, remember, we are not to ask as beggars and vagabonds, but as children who are heirs to the wealth of God's boundless resources! What we must constantly keep in mind, of course, is that these things are only for those whose prayer life combines this threefold form of asking wisely, seeking earnestly and knocking persistently.

J.B. Phillips once wrote: 'If you are writing a poem and the rhyme won't come and the lines just will not fit (or whatever dire problem you may have) . . . you may cry — 'William Shakespeare, help me'. . .and nothing happens.

'You may be feeling jittery, anxious over something, and you think of some great hero say like Nelson and cry — 'Oh Horatio Nelson help me'. . . but again not the slightest response. But if you are trying to live the Christian life . . . and have no moral strength and you cry — 'Jesus Christ help me', *something does happen*, at once just like that. There is a Living Spirit immediately available, and millions have proved it.'

We can learn much from men and women of God who were great in intercession.

Hannah prayed, 'Remember me, and not forget thine handmaid, but give unto thine handmaid a man-child . . .' Eli encouraged her, 'Go in peace: and the God of Israel grant thee thy petition.' And she received her request.

David's experience was that 'The Lord is nigh unto them that call upon Him.'

Jeremiah said, 'I cry night and day for my people.'

Hezekiah 'went up into the House of the Lord and spread it (a threatening letter) before the Lord'. And God delivered them!

Daniel 'went into his house . . . kneeled upon his knees three times a day, and prayed, and gave thanks.' The result — danger, suffering, but eventual elevation, revival, outstanding miraculous success!

In the New Testament, Jesus prayed. The lonely figure in prayer is a common picture. His disciples followed his example, for they asked, 'Teach us how to pray.' Peter later, long after Jesus had ascended into heaven, kept this habit of prayer. Acts 10:9 tells us, 'Peter went up upon the housetop to pray about the sixth hour . . .'

Through prayer we have the Lord's personal guidance. David claimed, 'He leadeth me . . . though I walk through the valley of the shadow . . .' We often ask many questions when we pray. Shall I move house, shall I emigrate, shall I invest money, shall I buy property, shall I retire now or later, shall I change my job, shall I get married? God wants to guide us at all times!

If we do not lose heart, the most difficult requests can be answered. God said, 'Neither will I hide my face any more from them, for I have poured out my Spirit' (Ezekiel 39:29). 'And shall not God avenge his own elect, which cry day and night unto him, though he bear long with them?' (Luke 18:7) This is the sort of prayer C.H.Dodd called 'the Divine in us, appealing to the God above us'. We must not be ashamed to ask for direction.

A pilot from the Port of London Authority went out to bring a large tanker into harbour. The captain asked him if he really knew where all the rocks were on the route to the port. 'No,' he replied, 'but I know where they aren't any!' Prayer keeps us clear of the rocks that destroy life. Prayer is guidance.

'Guide me, O thou great Jehovah' we sing. But do we expect it?

God uses the common and ordinary to guide us. An old man quoted a verse to back this up and to encourage someone who thought he could not do anything worthwhile:

> No doubt you can serve the Lord,
> with gifts so small and few,
> Remember the mighty oak
> was once a nut like you!

Yes! God guides nuts!

In G. B. Shaw's play *St Joan*, Robert de Baudricourt argues with Joan about her voices and pours scorn on her mission, arguing that God could not personally guide her.

> De Baudricourt – 'How do you mean voices?
> Joan – 'I hear voices telling me what to do, they come from God . . .'
> De Baudricourt – 'They come from your imagination.'

Joan – 'That is how the messages of God come to us all in our minds . . .'

God told Isaiah, 'I am the Lord thy God which teacheth thee to profit, which *leadeth* thee by the way thou shouldest go.'

The Psalmist sang, 'Thou shalt guide me with thy counsel, and afterward receive me to glory.'

Jesus taught us that 'the sheep hear his voice: and he calleth his own sheep by name, and leadeth them out . . . and the sheep follow him: for they know his voice.'

Thomas à Kempis wrote, 'Blessed is the soul which heareth the Lord speaking within . . . and receiveth from his mouth the word . . . and those ears which listen . . . for the teaching and truth within.'

When I am travelling in different parts of the world, down in the jungles of South–East Asia, in India, in the Australian Outback, or among the Zulus in South Africa, I may be in some remote part of the world, but now by modern communications I can lift the phone, dial direct and talk to my darling wife, whom I may not have seen for weeks, or my boys, and hear their voices. Through prayer we can dial direct to our Father. God directs and guides as we use the 'hot-line' to heaven!

Often when I write a letter I pray . . . when answering the phone I am praying . . . when I make a visit I pray . . . on a train, bus, driving the car, on an aeroplane. (It's surprising how often in mid–Pacific or over India in a typhoon passengers get interested in prayer – especially when the plane drops 3-400 feet in a few seconds!) You can pray God will lift your worries in business, help you with awkward workmates, meet you in your daily cares, heal that headache, calm the kiddies, resolve your deep problems, bless your minister, revive your church . . . Pray through the day every odd moment. Delight in it! Move in it! Begin to do it! God's orders to his Church are still the same: 'Ask and it shall be given unto you.'

'Ye have not because ye ask not' . . . Take prayer really seriously. John Knox prayed all evening then into the night and won 500 souls the next day.

Perpetual prayer is not only moving God in my direction. It is really moving me in God's direction. It is about changing *me*.

1 Chronicles 4:10 mentions an obscure but notable man of the Old Testament. There are 500 'begats' in that book, all different names, and with most of them we know nothing about their character, their life, their achievements or their lack of them. Suddenly it lights up. 'Jabez called on the God of Israel, saying, Oh that thou wouldest bless me indeed, and enlarge my coast, and that thine hand might be with me, and that thou wouldest keep me from evil, that it may not grieve me! And God granted him that which he requested.'

He prayed, he was specific and to the point. Out of these 500 people he prayed pointedly and sincerely and named his need, without doubt or shame. He asked—that is all there is about him in the Bible, but he is remembered to this day, thousands of years later. He is lit up among a whole generation by his prayer.

It is prayer real and true that the flesh detests, but the Spirit of God can use. It can lift us out of the carnal, natural man, into the spiritual realm. God can reveal things to us, cause us to overcome, enable us to move in the heavenly graces, gives us power, show us the truth. Prayer can ease tension and bring a sublime sense of peace. Walking in God's presence we are unmoved and untouched by the shakings around us. It works, it braces you, it girds you, it empowers you – the intercessor!

You want health? Pray for it till you get it! You want financial security? Why not pray for it till you get it! You want a Spirit-filled life? Pray for it till you get it! You want a life filled with joy abundant? Pray for it till you get it! You want to do something really worthwhile in life? Pray till it comes to you!

Pray big prayers and you'll get big answers!

The power of God is beyond comprehension. When we begin our meetings and urgent, earnest prayer has been made, no wonder blind people see – like the lady born blind in Lancashire who was interviewed recently on ITV after her healing. Seventy years blind and now she could see—through prayer in one of our meetings. As we pray together the power of God is manifested!

How much we can achieve when we are orientated in prayer. So why do we pray so little? We need to sort out our priorities.

On my way home from a large crusade service in England I may be driving at night through the centre of a town or city. I see people coming out of night clubs and discos in their droves, at perhaps 3 a.m. or later. If worldly people can spend all night in such places, ought not God's people to be spending all night in prayer meetings, bringing Revival by their intercessions? We used to sing 'sweet hour of prayer', we now say, 'Let's have a *word* of prayer . . .' then complain if we don't get much blessing!

Prayer is personal, powerful, exciting. It is not a monologue—it is a dialogue with God! We must picket God! Ask, seek, knock. 'For *everyone that asketh receiveth* . . .'

How many have found that in their moment of trial, prayer makes all the difference.

—The Christian minister with some intense church problem – prayer works it out.

—Some teenage child that is so rebellious, the situation seems impossible – then all is put right after prayer.

—A phone call in the middle of the night – I have had it so often – a heartbroken sob, someone's world has fallen in – we pray, and in ten minutes things are so different!

—That knock on my front door, some tearful daughter or mother – into my office we go, after seeking God, a smile, the answer!

—The long queue of people waiting to get into our meetings, thousands sometimes in the lines waiting for prayer and for counsel—so many go away, telling me later they got the answer to their need that night!

What power there is when we touch God by prayer. Paul went aside into the Arabian desert for three years and there he learnt to pray! The rest of his life became a fruitful ministry. Dr Yonngi Cho lay ill in a hospital bed, depressed and about to give up the ministry. It was his darkest hour. Here while set aside in prayer God spoke to him, and gave him the vision for the cell system, with its unlimited potential for growth in the local church. He arose refreshed and revived, a new man – and built the largest church in the world.

The angels must be dumbfounded because we have such power potential in our hands and *we pray so little*. Double up in your prayer life and you will double up in the blessing in your life. Tensions ease, difficulties are conquered, foes become friends, impossibilities are soon done, unaccomplished feats are soon in your grasp!

Here is the recognisable line of blessing – God prospers, uplifts, uses those who pray. It's the simple truth in this dark age. Instead of being overcome and swallowed up by the spirit of the age, destroyed, beaten, robbed, deceived by the thief out of hell, instead of being submerged by the stress, anxiety, frustrations of our times, the praying man gets results. He becomes God's winner!

'Very few of God's people really pray any more', wrote David Wilkerson. 'Ministers especially have become so busy doing Kingdom work . . . there is no time to pray and even less prayer in the Congregation . . . We can make time for anything we really want to do. Oh God, somehow get this generation on its knees!'

It takes effort of course and unusual dedication to be one who prays and gets results. Often I pray into the night, in fact much of my praying is done in the midnight hours. All noises have gone then – except on the Malaysia and Thai border, where it seems noisier at night in the jungle than in the day!

Randolph Churchill, son of Winston Churchill, loved to quote to his father Longfellow's famous verse, which we could spiritualise to mean powerful praying that costs:

The heights by great men reached and kept
Were not attained by swollen flight,

But they while their companions slept
Were toiling upward in the night.

'If we prayed twice as much and preached half as much,' claimed Derek Bingham, 'we would have Revival.'

Susannah Wesley raised 17 children. She brought them up almost alone while her husband was almost continuously away. She fed them, educated them and raised the two greatest social and spiritual figures of the seventeenth century, John and Charles Wesley, who 'saved' England with their loving, powerful Gospel preaching. It is said that she 'prayed in her apron'—in the midst of pressure and hustle and bustle, she stopped to pray, and she lived in prayer victory.

Browning had it partly right, I think, when he wrote, 'But God has a few of us whom he whispers in the ear, the rest may reason . . . Why?' It is because not enough of us desire him long enough, and persist with integrity earnestly enough. We do not take the time to learn the art of prayer, and we do not get to know the marvellous truths of the pathways of prayer. C. H. Dodd called this deep intercession 'the divine in us appealing to the God above us.'

Often we find ourselves unable to sum it up in words, like the little boy kneeling in prayer muttering 'A,B,C,D,E,F,G,H . . .' His brother heard him and asked him what he was doing. 'Praying,' he replied.

'You are not,' said his brother. 'You are just repeating the alphabet.'

The little lad replied, 'I do not know what to say to God, so if I repeat the letters of the alphabet God will take them and put them together into prayer for me, and then answer my prayer. He knows what I need!'

Yes, he knows what we need – 'He helpeth our infirmities', and there are unthought-of blessings, rewards, answers, fruitfulness through intercession.

I remember someone telling me they heard an old ex-convict pray. He was amongst a crowd of Christians all praying for the blessing of a big rally, including many well-known speakers and educated people. This old ex-convict prayed, 'Here, Lord, I wanna have a word in your ear. You and me's got to get together, Lord, for there's these 'ere people getting fed up waiten out there , . . It's about time O Lord you got a move on . . .'

Simple? Yes, but not irreverent. It was from the heart. God loves *real prayers*!

George Whitfield saw the value of real prayer warriors. He took a little crippled man with him everywhere who could not straighten his legs. This man's job was to pray day and night behind Whitfield. No wonder his sermons rocked England.

Lindsay Glegg, the great old English preacher, when well into his 90s, told me about the rough, tough, blunt old evangelist W. P. Nicholson, who once stayed in his home. He was a rough diamond that God had marvellously changed. He was amazingly successful in drawing vast crowds, winning tens of thousands of converts. Lindsay Glegg told me his wife once went into Nicholson's bedroom to tidy up and found his bedsheets all torn into shreds! It seemed he had been wrestling with God all night and obliviously as he knelt, tore the sheets in his very strong hands as he prayed! No wonder he had great power from God and drew huge numbers to Christ to find new life in him.

Charles Finney never took a song leader with him like most other evangelists did. He had a Prayer Leader, the Rev. Nash. He would find a quiet place away from everyone, perhaps in the woods, and secretly pray for Finney. No wonder he had mighty results!

In Auckland, New Zealand, where my campaigns have made such an impact on the media and drawn thousands to the services and produced such amazing cases of miraculous healing, an elderly lady, Jean Baughanis is always there praying. When I arrive for the meetings, if I get talking to people for long she knocks on the door of my room, or taps me on the shoulder at the entrance to the auditorium and reminds me, 'It is time to pray'! No wonder Auckland and the Islands have been stirred by the news of God's movings!

Evan Roberts, that strange, reclusive young man who spearheaded the Welsh revival, swept his way up and down the Welsh valleys, sometimes not even preaching, just weeping and praying. In Neath he spent a week in prayer without leaving his lodgings. Revival rocked the district and packed the churches, although no one saw the revivalist all the week! He paid the price in tears and prayer.

Don't make prayer a marathon—get to the point. Don't be repetitious like the Pharisees. God knows what we need but loves to hear us ask.

Tell him of your longings – and, he will fulfil them.
Tell him of your temptations – and he will shield you.
Tell him of your wounds – and he will heal them.
Tell him of your discouragements – and he will get you over them.
Tell him of your vanity – and he will remove it.

Prayer is a pleasure, not a pain! There is far too much formalised prayer in evangelical circles, but prayer should not be a boring chore. Prayer is a delight as we make our requests known to our loving Father.

As you begin to pray you realise your true position in the Family of God, as a citizen of the king, as a servant in the household of faith, and as a soldier in the invincible army of the king.

Pray for the right things and pray right! Ask God for right things and ask right! *Miracles happen through prayer.*

God has helped many in business through prayer. I prayed for a young man in Germany who was in bad need of a job asking God to inspire him with creative thoughts, lead him forward, and make it work for him. That young man now owns his own beauty and health aid company selling unique lines never before thought of all over Europe! He has put tens of thousands of marks into the work of God in that country.

I prayed for a woman who was worn and torn by care and worry, schizophrenic in mind, in and out of mental homes. Today she is an elder's wife, holds down a good job, and has not been back to a mental institution (from which she was previously rarely away) for 20 years!

Prayer can lift your heartaches.
Prayer can get you through next week.
Prayer can meet your daily cares.
Prayer can resolve your impossible situation and problems.

A girl who came for prayer in one of my meetings had an occult scar on her face which nothing bar plastic surgery could remove. Nothing would cover it or get it out. Months later it could not be seen as skin had grown over it!

The God of prayer is the God of miracles.

When the transistor radio first came to Africa a young man smashed his set against a rock shouting, 'Talk, talk, talk to me, they said you could talk . . .' His problem was that he didn't know how to tune it in. In his ignorance he was demolishing a really effective tool. Many folk I have counselled with anxiety-riddled lives have never really talked to God or tried prayer for any length of time. Some consider it a fantasy. But science has shown that prayer performs miracles in human personality.

A famous American psychologist said, 'Prayer is the greatest power available to the individual in solving his personal problems, its power astonishes me.'

Events take place that could only happen through the miraculous in answer to prayer. Archbishop Temple when told by an unbeliever 'All this prayer is coincidence' replied, 'It's funny, when I don't pray there are no coincidences, when I do pray coincidences happen.'

The real purpose of prayer is to draw you closer to God so that he can fulfil his will in your life. Many people fail in prayer because they are obsessed simply by getting what they want. Such prayer is doomed to failure. It is not designed to move God to our will, to get him to do all we want but to draw us for our good to *his* perfect will.

We need first to pray for cleansing from guilt and to yield ourselves.

Frank Laugbach said of prayer, 'Prayer is not a bucket but a fountain head. It is designed to connect your life . . . to God that His loving spirit flow through us.' To bring glory to him, help to ourselves and blessing to the world around us—that is prayer's purpose.

Prayer changes you as well as things.

Dr Alexis Carrol, a Nobel prize winner for medicine, said about prayer: 'It is the most perfect form of energy one can generate, its influence on the human body can be measured in terms of increased physical buoyance, greater intellectual vigour, moral stamina, and deep understanding of the realities underlying human relationships. I would say the truest life is literally a prayer, and true prayer is a way of life!'

Health-producing, power-generating, re-creating, love-exercising prayer is the kind that is filled with dynamic optimism, hope, faith.

We must learn praying of this type. And learning to pray is no light undertaking. If prayer is the greatest undertaking upon earth, we may be sure that it will call for a discipline that corresponds to its power.

Make up your mind at the beginning, if you are starting out on the prayer-life, that it will really cost you to pray, for the reason why so many people do not pray is because of its cost. They will not pay the price.

There is no other way of really getting to know God. Let that thought spur you on. We do not want to guess God: We must know him. Therefore, 'Be not weary in well doing'. Do not give up prayer because you are weary of it. Whenever prayer becomes distasteful it should be a loud call to pray all the more. No man has so much need of prayer as he who does not care to pray. Remember, also, that the great souls who became mighty in prayer, and rejoiced to spend three or four hours a day alone with God, were once beginners. They went from strength to strength.

If you feel it is difficult to learn how to pray, remember, you are not the first one who has faced the difficulty! Even Christ's chosen disciples were faced with the same perplexity, and cried out in agony of soul: 'Lord, teach us to pray!' Listening to Christ at prayer awoke a desire in them to be able to pray. Yet when they wanted to pray they found that they did not know how. They felt that they needed some orderly form by which they could speak to God out of their hearts. And he met their plea by giving them a form of prayer, which we call 'The Lord's Prayer'.

But we must guard against the peril of mere recitation in prayer, when we use such forms. It is not other people's prayers that make a man of prayer. It is possible just to 'say' prayers, and not to be really acquainted with the art of prayer at all. Doubtless, Saul of Tarsus had prayed many prayers right from the time he was a boy, but he never really 'prayed' until Jesus met him on the road to Damascus. The secret of Elijah's prayer was that he 'prayed in his prayer' (literally translated), that is, it was not a poor imitation of someone else, but it came right out of his own soul, boiling-hot!

There is no hard and fast rule of how to do it. The only way to learn to pray is by praying. This chapter and the many other books that have been written on prayer can only show you how to approach it. It cannot pray for you, nor can it teach you to pray. No reasoned philosophy of prayer ever taught a soul to pray. If you want to become a man or woman mighty in prayer with God and to get results, you will have to take time to do it, and to let God's Prayer-Teacher, the Holy Spirit, initiate you into the secrets of the prayer-life. Hurried prayers never produce souls mighty in prayer.

Tap into God's promises to bless our prayers. Take him at his word, like the old lady in the highlands of Scotland. A visiting minister, very well educated, preached on the words of our Lord's promise to never leave us nor forsake us and always to answer our prayers. Talking to this evidently simple little woman the brash preacher tried to educate her. 'Do you understand the

Hebrew meaning of the word "never", my dear?' he enquired. 'It actually reads in the original seven times, in other words, the Lord is saying to you he will never, never, never, never, never, never, never let you down.'

The little old lady looked up at the preacher and said, 'Ah, your reverence, for an intelligent man like you God might need to say it seven times, but for an old lady like me *once is enough*!' Yes, once is enough – take him at his word – ask, pray, knock, search and seek.

Here are what I call the ten commandments of successful praying:

1. *Have a definite hour for prayer, keep to it, avoid skimping, the earlier in the morning the better.* Wigglesworth found it better late at night, after midnight. John Wesley started at 4 a.m. for two hours every day.

> Blest be that tranquil hour of morn,
> And blest that hour of solemn eve,
> When on the wings of prayer upborn
> The world I leave.

2. *Have a definite length of time for prayer.*
An Eastern bishop kept a visiting high ranking Church official waiting an hour when he was in prayer. The visitor protested at being kept so long, but the bishop would not alter his hour for prayer.

Keep to that length, do not short-cut God. Always Bishop Ken was with God at 3 a.m. at the strike of the clock; Bishop Asbury at 4 a.m.; the early Methodist evangelists who changed England with their preaching kept strictly to 4–5 in the mornings and 5–6 in the evenings.

Dr Cho says no matter how busy he is he keeps his five hours in prayer daily. He told me how he had returned to Seoul early one morning after flying thousands of miles across the world from a preaching engagement, got into bed, slept for half an hour, and the phone rang. It was his mother-in-law reminding him that the people – 10,000 of them – were waiting for him to lead the prayer meeting. He jumped out of bed, changed, and as he walked on to the platform at Yoida Full Gospel Church, there was a burst of laughter from the thousands. His pyjamas could still be seen sticking out of the bottom of his trousers! But he got there!

Payson wore the floorboards away into grooves with his much praying.

Marquis de Party told his servant to call him after half an hour of prayer. The servant peeped around the door, saw the marquis' shining entranced face and did not call him till one and a half hours later. The marquis said, 'That was a short half an hour'!

It was said of William Bramwell, the holiness preacher, that he was more on his knees than off them!

Two ministers' wives were sitting on the veranda of a Canadian house, chatting to each other as they mended their husbands' trousers. 'I can't understand,' said one of them, 'why your church is always prosperous, while ours is not.'

'Well,' said the other wife, 'if you were an observant person, you would have noticed that I am patching these trousers on the knees whereas you are patching the seat.'

Samuel Chadwick, that great Methodist stalwart, used to say: 'The one concern of the Devil is to keep Christians from praying. He fears nothing from prayerless studies, prayerless work, prayerless religion. He laughs at our toil, mocks at our wisdom, but trembles when we pray.'

3. *Have a definite place of prayer.*

In Matthew 6:6, Jesus told us to find a place, 'and when thou hast shut thy door, pray to thy Father which is in secret'! John Mackenzie shook Scotland after his prayers at the mouth of the Lossie River. D. L. Moody used the back of the cobbler's shop in Chicago, praying, 'Here is my poor vessel, fill it with thy grace . . .' Revival came after the prayers of David Brainerd out in the Alaskan snow.

I like to use the bottom of my garden, in the summer

house, away from the telephone. I find God so often there away from it all!

Susannah Wesley found time to 'pray in her apron' while bringing up 17 children with no mod. cons. Today some with dishwashers, cars, microwave ovens, fridges, vacuum cleaners and only one child cannot find time to pray for five minutes a day!

But *we can* do it! If we do not we are lacking in desire and earnest longing for God and for fullness of life.

Go to your place of prayer, much, often, earnestly.

4. *Speak aloud in prayer.* Form words, rather than just thinking in the mind. David called on God, Abraham spoke to God; the early Church with many words sought the Lord.

When I speak aloud in prayer I find the reality of his presence seems all the greater. Remember God is near to you, so talk to him naturally.

David Wilkinson spoke about attending a Kathryn Kuhlman meeting and being led by the steward to her room, prior to the service. The steward left him in the passage. As he reached her room he stopped outside for some minutes with his ear against the door and could hear her audible cries to God to give her power for the multitude of sick people, 7,000 of them, who awaited her ministry in the huge auditorium.

Here are some great prayers that shook the world.

George Whitefield, the famous English evangelist, prayed: 'O Lord, give me souls, or take my soul!'

Henry Martyn cried as he knelt on India's coral strands: 'Here let me burn out for God.'

David Brainerd, missionary to the North American Indians, declared: 'Lord, to Thee I dedicate myself. Oh, accept of me, and let me be Thine for ever. Lord, I desire nothing else; I desire nothing more.' The last words in his diary, written seven days before he died, read, 'Oh, come, Lord Jesus, come quickly. Amen.'

Thomas à Kempis said to God: 'Give what Thou wilt, and how much Thou wilt, and when Thou wilt. Set it where Thou wilt and deal with me in all things as Thou wilt.'

Martin Luther prayed on the night preceding his appearance before the Diet of Worms: 'Do Thou, my God, stand by against all the world's wisdom and reason. Oh do it! Thou must do it. Stand by me, Thou true, eternal God.'

Praying Hyde, a missionary in India, pleaded: 'Father, give me these souls, or I die.'

5. *Pray in 'circles'.* Remember, God is the centre of all our prayers. Worship him first. Thank, adore, praise him. Magnify his name. Get close to him. As you get close to the centre, Christ, you will become confident, satisfied, strengthened, and you will pray well for others.

Some Christians tell others what they need rather than ask and receive. Pray for family, friends, children, national needs, church, minister and elders, missionaries, lost neighbours, and so on. What scope there is in the ever-widening growth of God's kingdom. Write down needs, make a list. Keep your promise when you tell folk you will pray for them.

6. *Seek to feel God's presence in prayer.* Even as you follow your prayer list, seek the Spirit's anointing. The Holy Spirit will reveal Christ as guide, empower our prayers, inspire our faith. Then with our hearts warmed by divine love we can name our requests with utter confidence and see them all happen!

All outstanding men of God have been known for their praying. Issac, Jacob, Moses, Samuel, Nehemiah, Daniel, Paul – all majored in the school of prayer. Prayer makes men God-like; their lives reflect his glory, their hearts throb with his love.

7. *Learn to listen.* No habit is more rewarding than silently waiting. We will talk more about stillness later. Let the Spirit search our hearts, purifying our motives, helping us to humbly accept our limitations while seeing his unlimited powers.

8. *Read your Bible alongside prayer.* Life-giving, purifying, faith-inspiring, it is the only textbook needed in your place of prayer.

9. *Cultivate believing prayer*. Faith expects something will happen. Refuse to be discouraged. Your stresses, worries and dire problems can vanish by such trusting intercessions.

An old epitaph reads:

> Here lies the body of Anxious Care,
> Who died of an overdose of prayer.
> He proudly continued a saint to tease,
> Until that saint fell on his knees.

10. *Persist, persist, persist*. This is the hardest lesson of praying. It is the greatest one to learn. Most unanswered prayer results from lack of it. We must stir ourselves to stick in there. Remember the death-bed words of the great missionary Adoniram Judson, apostle to Burma: 'I never prayed sincerely and earnestly for anything, but it came. At some time, no matter how distant a day, somehow, in some shape, probably the last I should have devised, it came.'

I have found these ten tips have given me sustenance, power and joyful living, as I have prayed and received God's answers thousands of times.

Finally, what is the spiritual secret of prayer? In my experience it is that *stillness is vital*.

Jesus showed a restful, peaceful, calm spirit, whether handling crowds and masses of people, schooling his men in private, taking them through a furious storm on the sea, encountering a madman, raising the dead, healing multitudes of sick people, meeting face to face the critics and the carnal debaters. He went on and on with unbroken calm and tranquillity amidst toil, heat, suffering, misunderstanding. He was never breathless, never anxious or disturbed, never hurried.

He left with us this greatest gift– *his treasured stillness*.

Longfellow put it so aptly: 'Let us labour for an inward stillness and inward healing . . . that perfect silence, where the lips and heart are still . . . where we no longer entertain our own imperfect thoughts and vain opinions . . . God Himself speaks in us and we wait and seek to do His will and do that only.' You will only know frustration and lack of power in prayer without this inner rest.

Your life is enriched in the quiet place. You become easier to work with, greater to be with, happier to live with, a blessing to share with. So *sit in God's presence. Let him flood your heart.*

Jesus said of Mary, when she was relaxed and listening at her Master's feet, while Martha was fretting and fussing: 'Mary has chosen the better part, and it will not be taken from her' (NEB).

Before a healing service I give strict instructions that no one must visit the vestry, dressing room, hotel, motel or minister's home where I may be preparing. I am still before God. He so often speaks to me with power in that place. I feel him near, sometimes I can sense someone standing by me. I so often hear to God's whisper.

Rider Haggard's mother brought up seven sons, without ever raising her voice to them. She explained, 'With seven noisy sons in the house, shouting would not do a bit of good. I found a whisper was much more effective!'

Go into a quiet place, do not talk, keep your body still, and listen. William James said, 'It is as important to cultivate your silence power as it is your word or tongue power . . .'

God's healing quietness can be experienced anywhere. I can be in a teeming city and find that quietness, or deep in the jungle in Malaysia, kept awake all night by the parrots and insects!

I can be among the throngs of India, the dormant suburbs of Moscow, the peaks of Mount Cook in New Zealand, in the Australian bush or the Gold Coast of Queensland, or among the masses of Zulus in Natal in a poor shanty town. In all these places, from the quietness deep in my spirit arises the confidence of God's Word and promises. But I can be in beautiful countryside and not feel it. The place is irrelevant.

70

Those silent moments are not apathetic escapism or a delusion. They are creative, dynamic, confidence-boosting. *'In quietness and in confidence shall be your strength'* (Isaiah 30:15).

In the silence put your problem in the hand of God. Think of it being solved in God's way, which is the right way. Believe that the healing peace of God is touching your mind, the blocks that have prevented guidance and anointing and power and victory from flowing through us are being removed, and let the answer float through to the top of your mind. How many times when tired and facing immense problems, and even somewhat tense, I have felt it all evaporate before me!

Do not be hasty, be still and wait. There is an old anthem that goes, 'There is a place of quiet rest – near to the heart of God.' Trapped in the vortex of modern life, we must get away from the noise, hurry and crowds with our harassed and fragmented minds and listen to God in stillness.

I like the '23rd Psalm for Busy People'. It goes like this:

The lord is my pace-setter, I shall not rush.
He makes me stop and rest for quiet
    intervals,
He provides me with images of stillness
Which restore my serenity.
He leads me in the ways of effectiveness
Through calmness of mind,
And His guidance is peace.
Even though I have a great many things to
    accomplish each day
I will not fret for His presence is here.
His timelessness, His all-importance will keep me
in balance.
He prepared refreshment and renewal in the midst
    of my activity
By anointing my mind with His oils of tranquil-
    lity,
My cup of joyous energy overflows.

Surely harmony and effectiveness shall be the
  fruit of my hours,
For I shall walk at the pace of my Lord,
And dwell in His house forever.

Among the great thinkers of history who have testified to the vital importance of contemplation and
quietness before God are Augustine, Madame Guyon,
Brother Lawrence, George Fox, Thomas Merton, David
Brainerd, Evan Roberts and many others. Dietrich
Bonhoeffer wrote: 'Real silence . . . really holding one's
tongue comes only as the sober consequence of spiritual
stillness.'

Dr Wilbur Chapman was once in a room with the
famous Praying Hyde. Hyde came in and turned the
key, locked the door, got on his knees, never said a
thing for five minutes. But Chapman said, 'Oh the Holy
Presence, just to kneel with him in silence, one could feel
God near . . .'

When Count Von Zinzendorf opened up his estate as
a haven for Moravian refugees, a building was set aside
for people to learn to wait upon God. It was called 'The
Lord's Watch'. A prayer meeting began there which was
to continue uninterrupted for 100 years. Later Moravian
missionaries influenced by that prayer chamber were
instrumental in leading John Wesley among others to a
firm commitment to Christ. Soon Wesley, Whitfield and
many others traversed Britain on horseback, preaching
the Good News and winning half the nation to Christ, in
what has been called the Great Evangelical Awakening.
They learned that waiting upon God gave them direction, strength, 'might in the inner man'.

A young man owned a Model T Ford. One day his
old car broke down. An expensive car stopped and a
distinguished gentleman stepped out. 'Would you like
me to help you?' he asked.

'No, I don't need your help, this is my car and I can
fix it, thank you.'

The stranger continued to watch as the young man
tried without success to get the car to go. Finally, he

looked up. 'All right, so what shall I do?' After a few minutes the man had the car running again.

'How come a rich man like you knows so much about cars?' the young man asked.

'I'm Henry Ford,' came the reply. 'I invented this car.'

There is nowhere better to get things right, to know the victory and to get answers, than listening directly to the Creator.

When Princess Anne returned from the Upper Volta in Africa, after seeing the poverty and famine and desperate need there, she said earnestly, 'Everyone go to church and get your prayer cushions out . . .' This is what we must do to succeed.

In one city in America, there is a phone number for tense people to dial, called 'Dial the Book'. The caller is given passages to read in quietness. Among the favourites is one that has helped hundreds, from Mark chapter 4. It tells about some men in a boat in a tumultuous storm, fearful, doomed, and very anxious. Then Jesus appears – kindly, relaxed, confident and calm. He speaks: 'peace be still' . . . and there was a great calm.

We too can experience in silent moments of prayer his outstanding power over our storms!

The soul that on Jesus hath leaned for repose,
I will not, I will not, desert to its foes;
That soul though all hell should endeavour to shake,
I'll never, no, never, no, never forsake!

As our thoughts are filled with God, stress drips away. He can enter into every part of our busy lives. The prayer goes:

Too often, O God, the sacred calm
Of your still small voice
Is overpowered by
The roar of the traffic,
The moan of ambulances,
The wail of sirens,
The growl of buses,

The rude interruption of the doorbell . . .
Jet planes, trucks, trams, TV, trains, telephones,
   motorbikes, transistors, ice cream vans with their
   chimes . . .
Let me know, O Lord, how to stop and pick you up!

A young Christian businessman got a big promotion
in his job. Asked how he hooked such a job so quickly,
he told his story. He had to meet a difficult customer
and try to land a strategic order for his firm. Before
the appointment he went aside to spend a quiet time
meditating, being still and praying about this challenge,
and the only quiet place he could find was the store room.
While he was there praying quietly before the Lord, his
boss burst into the room and asked with a suspicious tone
what on earth he was doing. He was the type of employer
who watched his staff with eagle eyes, keeping track of
all their working time.

The young man explained about the difficult customer
and the possible large order for the firm. He said he
wanted to pray and get composure and divine aid in
dealing with such a person.

The boss naturally watched him as he later dealt very
ably with the difficult customer. With winsomeness he
convinced him, and with confidence, care and courtesy
he won the order. Later the boss said with a smile,
'Perhaps I had better join you with that silent prayer
technique!' The Christian's success in his job was in no
small measure due to his prayer life, in which discipline,
control and spiritual quietness played a big part.

It is recorded that our Lord Jesus withdrew to the
wilderness and prayed . . . a great while before day he
arose and went to a lonely place . . . he went up into
the hills by himself (Luke 5:16, Mark 1:35; Matthew
14:23). We twentieth century workaholics need to turn
away from the chaffing pressure, mad scrambling and
panting feverishness we experience daily in our lives.

Pause awhile. Let your soul catch up with you. Give
time to things that matter. Do not be like the man in
Kleiser's poem 'Hadn't Time':

Hadn't time to sing a song,
Hadn't time to right a wrong,
Hadn't time to send a gift,
Hadn't time to practise thrift;
Hadn't time to see a joke,
Hadn't time to write his folk,
Hadn't time to eat a meal,
Hadn't time to deeply feel;
Hadn't time to take a rest,
Hadn't time to act his best,
Hadn't time to help a cause,
Hadn't time to make a pause;
Hadn't time to scan the sky,
Hadn't time to heed a cry,
Hadn't time to study poise,
Hadn't time to repress noise;
Hadn't time to go abroad,
Hadn't time to serve his God,
Hadn't time to lend or give,
Hadn't time to really live,
Hadn't time to read this verse,
Hadn't time – he's in a hearse –
He's dead!

We live at too intense a pace. We study, when we should meditate. We work, when we should wait upon the Lord. We dash, we fret at delays, we fume at disappointments, we lash ourselves into a flurry of activity – and accomplish little.

We must get away from the noise, bustle and crowds which fragment our minds, and listen to God in stillness.

Charles Wesley wrote, 'Breathe through the heats of our desire Thy coolness and Thy balm . . .'

Peter said, 'A meek and quiet spirit . . . is precious' (1 Peter 3:4).

'When he giveth quiteness, who then can make trouble?' (Job 34:29).

'Take heed, and be quiet' (Isaiah 7:4).

Elihu advised Job, 'Stand still, and consider the wondrous works of God' (Job 37:14).

Relax in a corner of the factory during tea or lunch break, read the Word and meditate. In the car during long journeys, turn in to a layby and sit quietly. Sit in a corner of the garden, or as I do in my little sunhouse at the bottom of the garden, or in a peaceful café with hot crumpets and coffee! *Be still*.

'My meditation of him shall be sweet,' rejoiced the Psalmist. 'I have . . . quieted myself.'

> Take from our souls the strain and stress,
> And let our ordered lives confess,
> The beauty of Thy peace.

A student visited a meeting of Friends (Quakers), taking notes for an assignment. After an hour of silence, she asked a person next to her, 'When does your service begin?' The Quaker answered, 'Now. We've just had our worship, now we're off to serve.' They discovered God's power in the stillness!

> Only to sit and think of God,
> Oh! What joy it is!
> To think the thought, to breathe the Name,
> Earth has no higher bliss!

When Christ talks to us in our stillness – his conversation and fellowship lift us.

It is in that place that we not only know God, but as Socrates said, 'We know ourselves'. Peter Sellers, the great comedian who died some years ago, was reported to have said, 'I don't have a clue who Peter Sellers is.' His wife Lyne Frederick said of him, 'He was in a constant state of turmoil about what his purposes on this planet were . . .' Prayer in quietness, listening to God, always eliminates such hopelessness.

In Psalm 4:4 David urges: 'Stand in awe . . . commune with your own heart upon your bed, and be still.'

C. S. Lewis spoke of the greatest possible evil society could suffer – are we close to it now? – the devil 'banishing all . . . silence . . . and filling it with noise.'

Martin Luther asked the question, 'All you who manifest an interest in religion – why don't you pray in the quite place?'

Wordsworth called it the place where we feel 'the trailing clouds of Glory'.

In the quietness it is helpful to *'prayerise, picturise* and *actualise'*.

1. *Prayerise.* Talk it over simply with God. Be still, listen, relax. If hindering thoughts persist so you cannot think enough of God, do what the Australian Bible teacher Dr F. W. Boreham did. He loved cricket, and when he went aside and tried to meditate he just saw the stumps, the bowler, the bat, the game. Finally when he prayed and thoughts of cricket intruded, he included it in his prayers – and it went! Relax, rest, let your swirling thoughts come to a stop, take time, read some apt words such as Psalm 1.

Pray without ceasing, but not always with words. Often I talk to God and get all my thanks and requests and my prayer list dealt with, then I leave all thoughts and problems with him and spend the rest of the time in silence, waiting for him to speak.

2. *Picturise.* I try to see a picture of what I pray for. When I bring a request, I see the person, problem, or need in my 'mind's eye'. I see, for instance, cripples dancing, laughing, skipping, running. I see blind people reading, talking and watching their grandchildren.

How many times have God's own dear children prayed with faith and confidence and then allowed the enemy to gain control of their imaginations. Instead of seeing a picture of victory, they see a picture of defeat. For instance, when you ask prayer for healing of your body, do you see yourself in the future healthy and happy, or do you picture yourself suffering and even having surgery?

Some people after much prayer over their finances picture new accounts coming their way, or unexpected money in the mail. Others, after praying, go their way planning in their imagination just how they will borrow the needed money, seeing their house and car repossessed if they do not obtain help. They are looking at all the alternatives if God does not come through by answering their prayer.

In Psalm 139:1–2 David says, 'O Lord, thou hast searched me, and known me. Thou knowest my downsitting and mine uprising, thou understandest my thought afar off.' Our thoughts are not hidden from God. He knows what you are thinking, even though your lips may be saying something else.

How do we use our imaginations to work with our prayers and not against them? How well I remember when God answered one of the first prayers I ever prayed for a material blessing. I was in desperate need of finance, with no church or friends or earnings support. At the very last minute every need was met!

But at the time when I asked God, I had a great sense of thanksgiving and rejoicing. I had already experienced the thrill of ownership in my thoughts – I had picturised it in faith!

Think of David. He saw Goliath not cursing a boy or even a king, not standing against a lad, but defying the God of Israel. In his mind he knew no one, but no one, could survive who cursed God. This giant was doomed.

In David's imagination he saw the stone sink deep into the forehead of Goliath and saw him topple. He did not see defeat – he only saw victory! It is this kind of thinking that works for you, not against you.

Jesus could see himself being killed by the soldiers; he could see himself being taken from the cross and buried. *He could also see something else.* What he saw is recorded in Hebrews 12:2: 'Who for the joy that was set before him endured the cross.' What did he see? He saw himself seated at the right hand of God the Father. He could see millions being redeemed from their sins. Encouragement for us in this realm is found in the words of Hebrews 12:3: 'For consider him [Jesus] that endured such contradiction of sinners against himself, lest ye be wearied and faint in your minds.'

What do you see when you pray? How far away is heaven? Does Jesus have a smile on his face as you pray—or a frown? Are things working for you, or against you? When you are in prayer, petitioning the Father, your mind will imagine either positive or negative thoughts and pictures. Hebrew 8:10 speaks of God putting his laws in our mind (imagination). God promised that he would put his promises in our imagination. If we have doubts and fears and wrong pictures of defeat, then God's promises are displaced.

Think in the stillness of Jesus. Fill your mind with the Living Christ, *see victory*!

3. Then in the silence *actualise*. Prayer shows us the part we must play. Resolve in the stillness to go and make it work, receive in the stillness the passion to carry it out.

One great thing that stillness achieves in our personal lives, apart from the vitality it adds to our prayer life, is to help us get our priorities right.

I wonder if you know A. A. Milne's amusing poem, 'The Old Sailor'? Shipwrecked, the old man begins to think of all the things he needs – water, clothes, a goat and some chickens, a hut to live in, a line and hooks for fishing, and so on.

He begins with the fish hooks, but as he starts to make them the heat of the sun reminds him that he needs a hat, so he starts to make that, but soon gets so warm that he goes in search of a spring to quench his thirst. Then he thinks of his need of animals and he is looking for these when he remembers that he needs a boat – which means making a sail, and to make a sail he must have needles, and as he is making these he thinks of his need for a hut . . .

> So he thought of his hut and he thought of his boat
> And his hat and his breeks and his chickens and goat,
> And the hooks (for his food) and the spring (for his thirst),
> But he never could think which he ought to do first.

It does help to get your priorities right if you are still!

Wait on God!
Wait for God!
Wait quietly in God!

Waiting like this in stillness, will bring satisfaction, peace, answers, power beyond compare!

One day in the late 1920s the Duke of York (later King George VI) was visiting a home for the old and homeless. There was great excitement amongst the old ladies, because they were to be photographed with the Duke of York. They wanted to include the family cat Sammy in the photo, with Wilson Carlyle, the founder of the Church Army, which ran this new home. But the cat could not be found anywhere. Just before he left the Duke went to see the Chapel. As he gazed around the small place of worship he spied curled up around the cross on the altar Sammy the cat, with his tail curled around the foot of the cross. Carlyle put out his hand to catch the cat, somewhat embarrassed, but the Duke stopped him saying, 'Leave him there, that is where we all should be!'

Resting in God, at his feet, is the place of power, reflection, inner solitude, victory!

Finally, this checklist gives guidelines for an effective prayer life:

1. Positively think about God.

2. Pray orally, with your own words.

3. Pray walking, travelling, at home, at school, at business, driving.

4. Affirm God's blessing, thank him, do not always ask.

5. Pray believing, sincere prayers expecting a rapid answer, but be patient in faith like Naomi who said to Ruth, 'Sit still, my daughter, till thou know how the matter will fall' (Ruth 3:18).

6. Never think negatively as you pray.

7. Accept his answers even if sometimes they are unpleasant.

8. In the silent moments put into his hands your problems, financial worries, family anxieties – 'take your burden to the Lord, and leave it there'!

9. Pray for those you do not like, for resentments are a blockage to power and effectiveness and can negate prayer.

10. Make a list of needs to cover and 'get it off of your chest' before the Lord.

11. Seek God, after your time of silence, with persistence regarding your needs. Remember 'Passionate persistence without impertinence produces progress!'

The place of stillness and rest at the feet of Jesus is the place of power and victory, the secret to praying the prayers that get results, and the triumphant door to Life with a capital L!

VI: *Get rid of stress and pressure*

When Paul wrote a letter to the church in Rome, he reminded them of the pressures about them that could destroy their faith. The same kinds of pressures are all about us. A different period in history has no effect at all. Sometimes the pressures are like a gentle nudge. At other times the pressures are as powerful as a vice, coming fiercely and relentlessly. 'I am come that they might have life . . . and have it more abundantly.' Many people lack energy, their vitality is low, they have inner conflicts which dissipate energy. What is the secret of energized life? Christ is the answer—it is said of him, 'In him was life'. Fill your mind with Christ, fill your heart with him. Let this mind be *in you* which was in Christ Jesus and inevitably, energy, vitality, exuberance, delight and eagerness will well up within you.

Turn to chapter 12 of the Epistle to the Romans and read verses 1 and 2. Here they are in Phillips' translation: 'Don't let the world around you squeeze you into its own mould, but let God remould your minds from within.' We are being, in Malcolm Muggeridge's words, 'hijacked by the world's stress factor', or as Paul put it 'squeezed by the world'.

People on every side are gripped by stressful and frightening situations today.

That squeeze tantalises and threatens the lives of young people. There is the power of drugs. There is the powerful wrong use of alcohol or the danger of becoming a compulsive gambler. There is the young fellow or girl who talks about free love and feels safeguarded by the abortion laws.

Older folk too are threatened by the squeeze of stress. They are tempted to stop bothering and stop caring. Their sense of mission in life diminishes and they feel that it doesn't really matter now what they do or how they react. Often they don't appreciate that as Dr Maurice Barnett put it 'a grave is only a little deeper than the rut they are in'.

Being a Christian means that through the discipline of faith we enter into an exhilarating exercise to resist the squeeze of the world. And by the power of the Christian Gospel we can have victory.

For the Christian is a person who has let God remould him. It is not that he overlooks the power of environment or circumstance. These powers are very great, but he has an inner renewing power.

The Christian is the one who has discovered the power which will break the fearsome pressures that tend to destroy men.

This power is God-power. It was the kind of power that Jesus promised when he said, 'You shall receive power when the Holy Spirit has come upon you.'

The ABC of the Christian Gospel is that our personalities can be invaded by the power of God!

Let me share with you what I have learned about stress in counselling and listening, from the Word of God, and from personal experience.

1. *Stress comes in the lives of people who are only existing and not really living*. Those who have no real purpose for living experience a vacuum in their lives. They turn to substitutes, and stress is the result. When you try to stuff into your empty soul that which never really satisfies, it brings exhaustion and exhaustion brings tension and stress. Nobody can live well – whether he is poor or rich – unless he has a rich meaning and purpose in life.

We have to have a reason to get up in the morning to go to work to come home and to go to bed to get up in the morning to go to work. When we don't have that meaning we turn elsewhere for inner satisfaction.

Too many times we have been deceived by the enemy and we begin to seek things to live with instead of something to live for. This is a sad mistake. Once we have the things to live with – possessions – and we discover that they don't satisfy, a restlessness comes. In that restlessness, there is stress and strain. There is still no rich, rewarding thing upon which we can base our hope. Life has to be going somewhere – without reservations or regrets. Without purpose stress sets in.

2. *Stress always stems from frustration.* Frustration simply means unfulfilled desires. We want things and when we can't have them we become frustrated. When we see that our desires and abilities do not match, that what life affords us does not compare with what we had hoped it would be, we get into the tug and tussle. We want and can't have, we seek but cannot achieve. We find ourselves slipping behind instead of going forward. Gradually, we see ourselves falling further behind and it frustrates us. We get tense and this results in physical and mental reactions.

People react strangely when things don't go right. I read in the paper how a mother of four in the USA decided one day that she could cope no longer with a house made untidy by four children. She would clean and in five minutes it seemed untidy again. One morning she gave up. She took her four children outside, went back in and set the house afire. It burned to the ground. That's one way of handling stress!

3. *Stress comes when we are constantly preoccupied with ourselves.* When we are consumed with what we want and what we like, we spoil everything we touch. We want – not because we need – but because we see that somebody else has. We're deceived into thinking that if other people can have certain things, we ought to have certain things also. We do not realise that just having is not necessarily a guarantee of happiness. 'Selfishness only causes trouble' Proverbs 28:25 (TEV). Out of this kind of thinking comes nervousness and restlessness. It is the state of many people far and wide today.

A German schoolmaster always bowed to the boys on entering his class. Other teachers laughed at him, but he said he respected the potential God put in those boys. 'You never know what those boys may become one day . . .' How right he was, one was Martin Luther!

Show respect. Think of others. Lose all selfishness. Forget self. Do not be occupied constantly with yourself. Lose stress by forgetting yourself. Show concern for others. Give kindness:

Kind hearts are the garden,
Kind thoughts are the roots,
Kind words are the blossoms,
Kind deeds are the fruits . . .

4. *Stress comes from resentment*. When you resent someone or something long enough resentment will turn into bitterness. If the root of bitterness goes deep enough, it will turn into anger. Medical experts tell us that resentment, bitterness and hatred affect blood pressure. This results in tension. I am told that continued resentment and anger will cause ulcers to develop. This is sometimes the cause of chronic fatigue, migraine headaches, and other nervous disorders. Resentment may even make our judgment perverted; it changes our mental outlook.

Many things cause us to feel resentful. Domestic problems in the home, tension between husbands and wives, unemployment and inflation—the list is endless. It is difficult to avoid everything which causes resentment. When we refuse to forgive or to leave the results of the situations in God's hands, resentment develops and stress is the end result.

Mrs Derek Prince tells the story of counselling a woman and urging her to forgive her husband, who had given her a miserable 15 years of married life. 'He's ruined 15 years of my life and you ask me to forgive him?' the woman cried.

Mrs Prince replied, 'Well, if you want him to ruin the rest of your life, just go on resenting him!'

How true, for the one who resents, suffers more than the one who is resented.

Jesus urged, 'Love your enemies and pray for those who persecute you' (Matthew 5:44, TEV). 'Whoever says that he is in the light, yet hates his brother, is in the darkness to this very hour' (1 John 2:9, TEV). Get rid of resentment. It is one of the most evil things in the world.

Harmonious living, peace and unity depend on right relationships at all levels. Resentment is the enemy that poisons the relationship between man and wife, between parents and children, families, class and class, church and church, nation and nation. Resentment buttresses the barriers between denominations and hinders friendship between Christians. The pride of the upper middle classes, the wealthy, and even the upper working class to those they think are 'below them' is a curse. The art of living together, of having peace, of moving towards greater equality will never be mastered till resentment is mastered. The ravages of this vice breed bitterness, depression and even disease. It causes nervous breakdowns and mental unbalance, it kills joy and fosters self-pity.

Jesus advised people to settle differences at once. 'Agree with thine adversary quickly,' he urged. He knew the danger of feuds and how resentments can burn in the heart for years and can be left like a legacy to succeeding generations.

Jesus loved men and women for what they could be. We too are judged by our godliness and holiness, on how we treat those who are of no earthly good to us and our ministries.

'You must rid yourselves of all such things as these: anger, rage, malice (resentments), slander . . .' (Colossians 3:8, NIV). To really live *you cannot nurse resentments or grudges*. They will poison you. One doctor claimed, 'Grudges and unforgiveness put the whole physical and mental frame on a war basis instead of a peace basis.' Dr Walter Alvarez said, 'I often tell patients they cannot afford to carry resentments or maintain hates, such things make them ill. I once saw a patient kill himself of it, inch by inch through hatred of a relative who had sued him. A year later he was dead.' Another doctor said a certain person had died of 'an undrained grudge'!

My wife Lilian really gets on well with people. She is very patient and tolerant. But two or three years ago, one person got on her mind. Every time she saw this person or thought of her, her blood would rise. In a healing line one night she asked the pastors to pray for her. To ask for healing from these thoughts and resentments was hard. Everyone knew her. She swallowed her pride. The fear and fixation disappeared, and the skin disease that had arisen at this time vanished overnight also!

If you bear a grudge you cannot see straight! As Chinese saying goes, 'He who spits against the wind, spits in his own face.' A man I knew said to a preacher friend who urged him to forgive a certain brother, 'I cannot, I will not forgive him.' He Later contracted cancer of the throat. The preacher visited him again, and urged him to forget the grudge. He died crying, I will never, never forgive him! Proverbs 26:4 (NIV) urges, 'Do not answer a fool according to his folly, or you will be like him!' Ephesians 4:26 says, 'Do not let the sun go down while you are still angry.' Resentments and grudges have no place in the heart of a true believer. You cannot enjoy life with them.

What did Jesus do to defeat resentment? *He forgave them.* Those rough soldiers on that crucifixion day expected the usual torrent of abuse and cursing as the nails went home, but from this prisoner came not condemnation but forgiveness.

Secondly, *he prayed for them.* Honest prayer scours the heart of hate. How can I get rid of deep resentment against someone who has injured me? Pray for him!

Thirdly, *he made allowance for them.* 'They know not what they do.' Pilate knew he was innocent, so did the priests. The soldiers suspected it—one was convinced and cried, 'Truly this was the Son of God'. But Jesus allows for them with kindly judgement.

Can you say of the drunken driver, the rapist, the faithless husband, the man who slandered you, the man who told lies and lost you a lot of business, 'They know not what they do . . .'?

Fourthly, *he served them*. Their wickedness could not defeat his love. He was as free to walk from the hill of Golgotha as he was from the mountaintop earlier when they were about to throw him off! He accepted death, and laid himself upon the wood. If he had drawn back, sin would have won. In the midst of their hate, he served them. He not only died *by them*, but *for them*.

How can I overcome resentment against certain people? Serve them—thoughtfully, deliberately, prodigally. Give ourself for them. 'Love your enemies,' commanded Jesus, 'do good to them that . . . despitefully use you.'

Stephen the first Christian martyr had learnt this lesson of conquering grudges. What a magnificent echo of Calvary! He followed the example of his Master as he was battered to the ground, crying, 'Lord, lay not this sin to their charge.' He had the mind of Christ—he had died to all grudges and resentments!

5. *Overwork often brings stress*. In Exodus 18:13–26 we have a classic case of overwork. Moses was burning the candle at both ends. His father-in-law saw what was going on and said, 'Moses, you are never going to make it. You are going to wear yourself out. Let me give you some advice.'

Moses replied, 'But I have to do this. This is my job. These people have disputes, they come to me and I try to settle them. It's my responsibility.'

What Moses couldn't see was that it was an impossible task. He failed to deal with his own limitations. Jethro saw that Moses was heading for a breakdown, that he couldn't continue to do all he was attempting to do without snapping under the load.

Life has its blind spots. It seems that people are increasingly thinking of work as drudgery. Some people even think work is a curse. Have you noticed what people who hope to win a fortune from betting often say? 'I am going to retire from my job.' Why do they say that? Psychologically, we have come to think that the obstacle to happiness is work. We see it as a burden, a form of torment. I have experienced this. If I had twenty lives to live, I would live every one of them for the ministry, but sometimes I find myself feeling that the tasks I have is unending. Even the ministry can become a burden because of the pressure of duties.

Moses was a prophet, a man of God, yet his father-in-law had to say, 'You . . . will wear yourselves out. The work is too heavy for you; you cannot handle it alone' (Exodus 18:18, NIV).

Overwork or a wrong attitude toward work is a source of stress.

6. *Stress also comes from worry, fear and anxiety.* I don't need to tell you this. You know it. We are afraid that somebody will find out what happened yesterday. Or we are afraid of what may happen tomorrow. Fear is inner panic. Fear allows the imagination to go wild. Fear causes our minds to be dulled and we get into a fog of confusion. Our hands become clammy, our throat becomes dry – we are under stress.

An article in *Time* magazine stated that it is not the big worries or the super fears that bring the most tension or depression, rather, it is the monotonous drip, drip, drip of everyday fears and worries and discouragements. The continuous pressures of little things gradually change our behaviour until we don't laugh any more. Everything becomes so serious. We begin to think every cloud has a dark lining. If the worst hasn't yet come, we feel it soon will. We begin to look on the dark side of life. Fear produces stress.

We know that 90 per cent of the things we worry about never happen, and the other 10 per cent we are capable of handling once they arrive. Yet we fear the unknown. As Harold Christy, the great American artist, put it, 'I so fill my mind with God, that there is no room for worry.' Tension even affects animals. In a big American city some time ago, it was reported that a great 60-pound Airedale dog suddenly dropped dead of a heart attack, when two small dogs barked loud at him just behind his back!

In Paris recently newspaper headlines ran— 'Traffic Affects Policemen's Nerves'. The report went on, 'Many of Paris's over 25,000 officers have developed cardiac conditions, as a result of the capital's nerve-racking traffic situations. Some 2,500 officers are absent from duty every day because of nervous exhaustion, after a day's work whistling, yelling and pointing their white sticks at erring motorists in Paris streets. . .'

Add to the noise the nightmare of queueing for planes, strap-hanging in packed trains and buses, driving through traffic-jammed streets, and the hectic tempo of life daily, and we are left with little energy to keep the lions of fear chained in the remote dungeons of the mind. In a sentence, there is 'too much going on'. Excitement, turmoil, rush and overbusyness infect even quiet homes. Speed is a demon worshipped by many. 'Let's move fast' seems the unspoken slogan which directs thousands of restless people.

St Theresa had it right: 'Let nothing disturb you . . . nothing afright you, everything is passing, except God. God alone is sufficient.' 'For God hath not given us the spirit of fear; but of power, and of love, and of a sound mind' (2 Timothy 1:7). You can be healed by this text. What power overcomes fear? Faith—the only force more powerful than fear. Affirm faith in the greatest power in the universe – Christ, the King of kings. Put complete trust, confidence, and complete dependence on the Lord. Practise this attitude and fear diminishes. Live in this relationship with God and fear vanishes, you develop a sould mind, and the shadow of fear cannot lurk near you.

Remember, God knows how much we can carry. He knows our heartaches, heartbreaks, temptations. He knows about our tensions; burdens, buffetings. He knows all that we face—distrust, resentments, doubts, cynicism, anger, indifference. David encouraged us in Psalm 37: 'Commit thy way unto the Lord; trust also in him; and he shall bring it to pass.'

7. *Stress comes from broken connections*. What causes

loneliness? A break of connection. When the connection is broken, life stops flowing. When life stops flowing the spirit becomes wounded. Your spirit can become as tired as your body. When this happens, it loses its lustre.

Some people break connection with themselves. That is, they have failed so often, or they have been wounded by circumstances, or been rejected or so deeply hurt that they don't like themselves any more. They are tense and stressed.

Others have broken connection with their families. They have allowed barriers to build up. They have isolated themselves. They are afraid to make friends any more. They are afraid they will be hurt again because they were hurt once in marriage. Or they made friends and shared confidences but were bruised and hurt when the connection was broken.

Sometimes the enemy deceives people in their old age. When there is no place to live but by yourself, when the children won't let you live with them or you have no children, when you are in a nursing home or senior citizen's apartment, you can feel, 'Because I am old I am useless, I am no good to anybody; I am a liability to society.' You then stay alone and isolate yourself.

You see, when we break connection with ourself or with our family or with our friends, then we feel unwanted. In the midst of a crowd of people, in a busy church, in a throng of people, it is easy to be lonely. Many people today are under stress because they are simply lonely.

8. *Stress stems from guilt*. When you do something to yourself or someone else that violates what you know is right, remorse sets in. Remorse or guilt brings a great deal of stress.

The world says, 'There is nothing that anybody can do when you make a mistake. It is in the past so forget it. Not even God can do anything about it so repenting is unnecessary and of no value. Don't cry over spilled milk.' This sounds good but it is not the truth. It is naïve and shows ignorance about human nature.

God has said in his Word: 'If we say that we have no sin, we deceive ourselves' (1 John 1:8). When God's laws are broken, they must be weighed on divine scales. We must measure our behaviour by God's measuring rod. We can forgive ourselves and we ought to, we can forgive others, and we ought to, but we must have divine forgiveness if we have broken divine laws. There is no forgiveness unless you ask God for it. How many people are under stress today because they have broken the moral laws of God and have not sought forgiveness from God. As a result they are suffering from stress. But 'if we confess our sins, he is faithful and just to forgive us our sins, and to cleanse us from all unrighteousness (1 John 1:9). And we shall be free of stress too!'

Now for six biblical steps to overcoming stress.

1. *Guard your prayer time*. Guard it as you do your meal time. You know how you get anxious if you miss your supper! In your quiet time, I suggest that you learn to relax – to loaf – in God's presence. Isn't that a neat phrase? Learn to loaf in God's presence. You can't hear his voice if you're in a hurry. You can't perceive his guidance if you are rushing. Don't focus attention on yourself, but renew your relationship with God. Enjoy his presence, unwind, find refuge in him. Get alone with God. Guard this time. Make it a priority in your life. It will give you balance.

2. *Speak often of God's power* throughout the day. Quote Scriptures such as, 'Greater is he that is in you, than he that is in the world' (1 John 4:4), and 'I am full of power by the spirit of the Lord' (Micah 3:8) Sing uplifting songs: 'There is power, power, wonder-working power, in the precious blood of the Lamb.' When you are tempted to become discouraged, encourage yourself in the Lord by quoting a verse of Scripture or reminding yourself of God's intervention in the past.

3. *Forgive and love your enemies*. The Peanuts cartoon in one comic strip showed Lucy telling Peanuts off for not liking others. He remonstrates with her, replying, 'I do so love mankind, it's people I can't stand . . .'

Nothing in this world is worth robbing you of the joy of living, of peace with God, or of goodwill toward men. Nothing! A man came into my office who needed counselling. As we talked, there surfaced in our conversation a deep hatred for one that he finally confessed was his father-in-law. I told him he had to get rid of this, that he must not only forgive him but also love him. Then I led him in a prayer. Three times, he broke down and couldn't pray his father-in-law's name. The fourth time he got through it.

As we talked I had noticed he appeared to have arthritis. I'm not a doctor but I did see that his knuckles were swollen and his fingers were cupped in. He had difficulty moving his fingers. I saw this when he reached for a tissue in his pocket. Nothing was said about it.

On his way home, he stopped at a telephone and called me. 'I've been doing what you told me to do. As I drove along, I not only thanked God aloud that he let me forgive my father-in-law, but I have been asking God to bless him. I prayed that I would truly love him. Do you know what happened, Pastor? The stiffness in my fingers is all gone. I can move them without effort. I'm having a praise meeting right here in this telephone booth.' Healing often follows repentance.

Now, I cannot promise that if you love and forgive your enemies, whatever is wrong in your body will *always* go away. I don't guarantee healing every time, but I can guarantee you a release in your spirit. When you love and forgive your enemies you will come alive and good things will begin to happen.

4. *Rebuild the connections*. Rebuild family relationships. Learn to like yourself. Come out of hiding. Don't die by yourself. Find love. There is somebody you can love and somebody who will love you. Come alive and rebuild those relationships – at any cost.

Fellowship is living together on the highest plane. It requires first the acceptance of each other, then the appreciation of each other. Some break fellowship on the ground of 'incompatibility'; but we are all incompatible as unadjusted individuals. Fellowship is the adjustment of our ego, pushing it off centre to make room for others. It is not easy to deny self its grasping for supremacy. Nevertheless it can be done. Oxygen and hydrogen are incompatible, but mix them in the right proportions and fire an electric spark through them and they coalesce—they become water (H_2O)! As Aaron Linford put it, 'The spark of divine love can take incompatible you and me and fuse us into a new entity—of one heart and one soul.' This is Christian fellowship!

I have seen thousands lose their debilitating anxiety and stress when linked in close fellowship with other Christians and with family and friends. When right relationships and harmony replace division and antipathy, the pressures of stress are lifted!

5. *Deal with problems quickly.* Act immediately. I must say I find this difficult. I like to put off unpleasant things if I can, for as long as I can! But it has brought much satisfaction and much less pressure to get problems, or 'looming' potential problems, over with as rapidly as possible.

Troubles early mastered can be used to our advantage, just as the same wind that drives a sailing boat towards danger can be mastered so as to take it to safety! Master problems rapidly, and stress will be cut by half. For difficulties can give way to peace, darkness to light.

St Francis recommended that when faced with the problems of living in an evil world, our reaction should be the opposite to that of the natural man. He put it this way:

Where there is hatred – sow peace!
Where there is injury – sow pardon!
Where there is doubt – sow faith!

God uses men to sort out problems! When Strasbourg was bombed, they found a statue of Christ under the rubble, with no hands. A famous sculptor offered to put new hands on it, but the church authorities refused, and you can see it today with no hands. It is a reminder of suffering, but also that God uses no hands but ours! He expects us to face up to and deal with our own problems – but offers wisdom and know-how to handle them.

Jane Taylor, who wrote the famous nursery rhyme 'Twinkle, twinkle, little star', penned another verse: 'How pleasant it is at the end of the day, no follies to have to repent, but reflect on the past and be able to say, that my time has been properly spent'!

How elevating, and how stress is reduced, if we can look back and say, I by the grace of God and the strength of the Holy Spirit got on top of that problem today. I did not waste time and undermine my health by letting tension and stress build up, I caught it at the right time!

Say with David, 'Thou hast enlarged me when I was in distress' (Psalm 4:1).

'In my distress I called upon the Lord' (Psalm 18:6).

'God . . . answered me in the day of my distress' (Genesis 35:3).

6. *Find forgiveness from God.* 1 John 1:9 reads: 'If we confess our sins, he is faithful and just to forgive us our sins, and to cleanse us from all unrighteousness.'

Recently, I looked into the eyes of a couple who were in a mess. It was such a mess that I said to myself, how do people tie themselves in such knots? The Scripture warns us that 'the devil, as a roaring lion, walketh about, seeking whom he may devour' (1 Peter 5:8). Do you know who the devil would like to devour? Each and every follower of Jesus Christ. He would like to devour me, he would like to devour you. He was clearly trying to devour this couple – and succeeding quite well. I said, 'I'll tell you what it will take. It will take seeking forgiveness from each other, from yourselves, and from God. You need to rebuild the connections. Start rebuilding your lives in a quiet time each day.' I looked them straight in the eyes and said, 'The choice is yours, it is up to you.'

The choice is always ours. 'ASK, KNOCK, SEEK, FIND.' As Peter said, 'You can rest the weight of all your anxieties upon him, for you are always in his care.' (1 Peter 5:7, J. B. Phillips). As Jethro said, 'If you do this

. . . you will be able to stand the strain and . . . go home satisfied.' No need to be squeezed, overcome, bullied by circumstances, or HIJACKED by stress. The pressures of life can vanish! Each of us must make the decision to change our lives. With God's help we can conquer stress.

VII: *Unlock your faith power*

Faith is power!

A story is told of Sir James Barrie, the famous author of *Peter Pan* and other great stories. He stayed in many homes on his lecture tours and theatre travels, and was well known for the little tricks he loved to play.

Sometimes he would gather the children around him in a household, and say, 'I can put a stamp on your ceiling.'

The kiddies would all say, 'Oh, no, you can't!'

He would then proceed to prove them wrong. He would get a big penny out of his pocket, then lick a stamp and lay it face down on the penny. With a clever twist and flick they would both go upward and hit the ceiling. The penny would come down, and the stamp stick there. Many houses kept that stamp there, and years later, when they boasted that the great Sir James Barrie stayed there, to prove it to unbelievers they would point to the famous stamp on the ceiling. 'We can tell he has been here,' they used to say, 'by what he's left behind.'

We can always tell where men of faith have been. They leave their mark for eternity. A great old man of God in Boston, Lincolnshire, back in the 1960s used to drive me sometimes to my crusades. He was a retired lorry driver, and in those early days I had no car, so he used to pick me up with all the literature, microphone, equipment, and gear and drive me miles. We used to talk on those long journeys around Britain on soul-saving and healing missions, and he often quoted that mighty man of faith, Smith Wigglesworth, whom he had known. Amongst the many gems he told me were these:

'Have the Word of God abiding in you if you want faith to be in evidence . . . Faith doesn't take any strength to carry, it carries you . . . Bring your mind to the Word of God, not the Word to your mind . . . Without faith you have nothing . . . Once you have laid hold of the plain lines of faith, the simplicity of faith leads you into a new world.'

Today we are in a faith battle . . . a faith struggle . . . a faith war. It demands all of us. 'Without faith God can do nothing with man' said Samuel Chadwick, 'and man can do nothing with God.' You may think you have a weak faith and cannot receive much from God, but that is at least a start. Some faith is better than none! A weak faith can become strong.

Years ago, an old farmer told me that as a boy he wanted to hear the great evangelist Gipsy Smith. It was the last time he ever preached at a large rally in this country before leaving for America just before the Second World War. His minister grumpily said, 'He is not what he used to be!' It put the young man off, and he never did hear the great man of faith before he died.

It's funny, when people don't like a preacher, or appreciate a certain personality, then it is always 'He's not what he used to be!' But faith is always improving us, changing us, empowering us, bettering us.

A few years ago a certain minister said of me, 'His missions are tailing off, he will be out of demand, no one will want him in another six months.' I have seen greater miracles of healing in the five years since then, and larger missions than ever before!

So do not be put off from advancing in faith. You never graduate from the school of faith. It is an unending lesson we are learning. So when people call you weak, or tell you you'll never make it, or you're untalented, remember they have said it all about God's fruitful people before you.

What is the great secret to unlocking faith power? The answer lies succinctly in the dynamic and creative teaching of Jesus Christ: 'If thou canst believe, all things are possible to him that believeth' (Mark 9:23). As you learn faith and train your heart and mind to believe, defeatist tendencies are reversed, and everything moves out of the area of the impossible into that of the possible.

The steps to unlocking your strong faith are four fold:

1. *Desire*. Alice in Wonderland protested to the Queen, 'One can't believe impossible things!' But God said we can. First we need to *desire* to. The founder of the game of rugby is commemorated with a plaque which says, 'With a fine disregard for the rules of football, he took the ball in his arms and ran.' We will never go ahead with God if we keep to all the respectable rules of the game, if we accept the status quo around us, if we merely move in the same spiritual 'rut' and follow the same churchy traditional mould, and if we do not have desire for God and for strong faith! Do not inhibit your spiritual desires. Press ahead, seek God, stir up a desire that becomes a searching, for a heart that seeks after faith is rewarded! 'Desire spiritual gifts,' Paul urged.

Desire means defeating negativism. Rampant negativism is one of our greatest enemies— 'It can't be done . . . It won't work . . . I'm happy as I am . . . I'm too busy to think about these things.' Every time we speak in such a way we are denying the new birth Christ gave us. For Jesus was always positive. The most powerful men and women of faith are those who have overcome negative attitudes. When holy desire is in you,

no failure overcomes you
no circumstances overcome you
no financial problems overcome you
no party strife overcomes you.

2. *Submit yourself*. To submit means to take his hand, to put your full weight and reliance on him. A young boy (who was later one of Scotland's most famous High Court Judges) was hanging by his fingertips on the edge of a dangerous cliff. His life was in grave danger. Suddenly a hand appeared over the top, and a voice said, 'Take my hand.' He could not see who it was, but grasped the stranger's hand and was pulled to safety. That young lad submitted to his rescuer—he asked no questions, threw himself on the unseen deliverer and

grasped the hand. The hand was that of the young writer Robert Louis Stevenson – and the boy was saved.

Submit to God, take his hand. Go out with faith into the unknown with full surrender and reliance on him. In Dickens' book *A Tale of Two Cities* a little servant girl in Paris during the French Revolution, is about to leave the jail to go out to be guillotined. She is fearful and distressed. She turns to the hero Sidney Carton, who is innocent and going to his death in the place of another, and says, 'If it's possible may I hold your hand?' Hold God's hand. Give yourself away. Die within, that faith may live in you. Claim God's bountiful faith which is awaiting you!

Many today have mislaid the key that opens the door to the Kingdom—faith. Faith is a great force just waiting to be used. Faith realises that to our Heavenly Father all is possible.' 'He is able to do immeasurably more than all we ask or imagine' (Ephesians 3:20, NIV). William Barclay stated, 'Faith steps out on the seeming void and finds the rock beneath.' Faith launches out, works with utter abandonment on the promise, and seizes the object before it. Hesitation is doubt. Faith does not doubt or hesitate. Trust in the naked Word is like a sixth sense that taps into that other invisible unseen World. As David Watson said, 'You cannot trust God too much!'

3. *Nurture faith*. James spoke of those 'rich in faith'. Paul said, 'Add to your faith.' The disciples prayed, 'Lord, increase our faith.' Jesus said there was one with 'great faith'—so you can be at different stages. Paul urged, 'Let us fix our eyes on Jesus, the author and perfector of our faith.' The Greek here says, 'Fix your eyes on, looking away from and unto the pioneer of faith, Jesus.'

So as we look to him, faith can expand. The greater our knowledge of him and the Word, the greater will be our faith. As David Watson said, 'Our limitless trust in God seems to satisfy him,' and as J. Oswald Chambers said, 'The function of faith is to turn God's promises into facts.' Faith can aid us in uprooting whatever obstacle is between us and the will of God. 'Faith brings a man empty to God,' said John Calvin, 'so he can be filled by him.'

A little saying I often use in my meetings goes, 'Faith never stands around with its hands in its pockets.' For faith sees the invisible, believes for the incredible, and receives the impossible.

The motto outside a church in Missouri, USA, runs, 'We believe that the power *behind* us is greater than the task *before* us.' Nurture this kind of faith.

Faith is a philosophy of life which is diametrically opposed to the secular thinking of our age.

'To have faith is to be sure of what we hope for, to be certain of the things we cannot see' (Hebrews 11:1 TEV). It makes God real now.

I was being interviewed on a national radio programme and was asked, 'Isn't this faith business, Mr Banks, a shot in the dark, a sort of blind date, a leap into the dark?'

I leaned over towards the interviewer and replied, 'Sir, it's not a leap into the dark, it's a leap into the light!'

As we grow in faith we grow in the light of our heavenly Father, we gain experience in trusting God, we gain greater confidence and knowledge of him, and we know how to act in the situations that we face. Trust in God allows God to express his absolute power towards us. *Faith is the strongest power in the universe.*

Faith claims on the strength of what God states in his declared promises in his Word. God says he will give us all he has promised. *But you must take possession of it.*

John says in the last book of the Bible, 'Whosoever will, let him take the water of life freely . . .'

Reach out, grab it! Use your faith! Nurture your faith! Faith is one of the most prominent subjects in the Bible. The Christian life is called the life of faith. It is written, 'The just shall live by faith.' Throughout the Scriptures the Christian is exhorted to 'stand,' 'walk,' 'fight,' 'resist' and to 'overcome' by faith. There is also the joy of faith, the prayer of faith, obedience of faith, and so on. We are warned that 'without faith it is impossible to please him [God]' (Hebrews 11:6). But 'if ye have faith

. . . nothing shall be impossible unto you' (Matthew 17.20).

It is interesting to note that often Christ required some evidence of faith before he worked a miracle. Sometimes he demanded men to do the impossible, such as inviting the man with the withered hand (Matthew 12:13) to 'stretch forth thine hand'. The lepers were exhorted in Luke 17:14 to 'go, show yourselves to the priests' even when they were still lepers, but as they went they were healed.

How stimulating it is to read about the heroes of faith in Hebrews II. No part of the New Testament is more encouraging when we are confronted with trials, than this one. These dedicated men and women knew nothing about the spirit of defeat because they had a sense of the presence of God and their lives were controlled by the principles or righteousness. Nothing daunted them. We should learn to exercise our faith, like those who marched around the walls of Jericho until they fell, or like Moses who was told to 'go forward' when the sea was blocking his way. To overcome difficulties we have to exercise our faith, and we need to encourage one another. There is an incident in the Book of Acts where Paul perceived that a man had faith and he shouted a word of encouragement to him. 'Stand up,' said the Apostle. Fancy saying that to a cripple! But Paul saw that the man needed to put his faith into action.

Let us use our little faith that we might receive deliverance. How we need to believe the promises of Scripture and embrace them. We can do so if our lives are lived in conformity to the Word of God and when we are prepared to believe when we cannot see. This is the scriptural principle for seeing miracles in our lives. Jesus said to Lazarus's sister, 'Said I not unto thee that if thou wouldest believe, thou shouldest see the glory of God?'

People often say, 'When I see, then I will believe.' Jesus pointed out that it was the other way round. 'If you believe, then you will see!'

What we must also realise is that delays are not denials. The Bible makes this clear. Over and over again we see how God tried the faith of people like the woman of Canaan (Matthew 15:21), Jairus (Mark 5:22), Martha and Mary (John 11:3), and the nobleman whose son was sick (John 4:46). This man had to go away from Christ with just a word and believe what he told him. When he arrived home he found his son perfectly whole.

4. *Expect events to work together for good.* Wigglesworth said, 'Faith is the only way to all the treasures of God.' The word is used 490 times in the New Testament. Jesus 'rebuked them [his disciples] for their lack of faith and their stubborn refusal to believe' (Mark 16:14, NIV). *We must expect things to work out in response to our faith.*

Moses 'endured [overcame] by seeing him who was invisible [by faith].'

James claimed that 'the prayer of faith shall save the sick.'

Jesus said, 'Did I not tell you that if you believed, you would see the glory of God?'

George Muller, the great saint from Bristol, was on a voyage across the Atlantic in heavy storms. The captain warned that they would arrive late—possibly a day behind. Muller countered that they would be on time because in 57 years he had never yet been late for an appointment on God's business. The captain laughed, he thought Muller was mad.

Some time later, they sailed into harbour minutes *early*. The captain was astonished that they had caught up on time, but Muller told him quietly, 'My eye was not on the furious elements, but on God who controls the fury and all the circumstances of life . . .'

Living by faith is a great adventure. I have done it for 34 years, and God has never let me down. Men may let you down. But God never fails.

Someone wrote to Dr Billy Graham and asked, 'I try again and again to have faith, but I can't seem to achieve it. Can you help me?'

Billy Graham replied, 'Stop trying and trust. Faith doesn't come in the confusion of frenzied self-effort and vain striving, it comes when we stop struggling, when we let go . . . and rely on God.'

Faith rests on God's greatness, his sovereignty, his faithfulness. In spite of ups and downs and difficulties. In the 'Peanuts' cartoon, Charlie Brown has lost one game of football after another. Lucy sends him to a psychiatrist to get sorted out as he is depressed and defeated. He sits in the chair, and the psycho talks to him: 'You must see that life is made of ups and downs . . .'

Charlie jumps out of the chair and goes out screaming, 'I hate downs, all I want is ups . . .'!

We don't like the 'downs' or problem days, but these 'try' faith – they reveal what faith is.

John White put it: 'Faith is that . . . which continues to respond to the Word of God, in the absence of outward encouragement . . .'

In God's time, events will turn to good. God knows what is best for us and when to answer our cry.

What we often forget is that faith cannot operate in a void. We must have difficulties and uncertainties, barriers and obstacles, darkness and trials to enable faith to work. Any other kind of life would not be a life of faith and it would lose its excitement and interest.

The God who acts in response to faith is still with us in the twentieth and twenty-first century! Faith is not given to us for ourselves, however, it is given for the Kingdom to grow, for us to grow like Christ, for evangelistic power in the whole earth, because it lets mortal, ordinary men see a glimpse of the power of that other world, and see God work down on earth *today*!

Faith to the world looks so blind, futile, unreliable and small, a foolish and crazy way to act and live. I have seen people enter my healing crusade meetings bored, restless, sometimes mocking. Their faces show a complete lack of interest. Then suddenly everything changes as they see faith at work. I have seen people stand by aghast, shout praises to God, run to the altar to look closer at the miracles of God. They are filled with holy awe, some even weep at the signs of God's presence.

But how slow we are to learn. It was the same with the disciples of old. On four occasions Christ gave them a gentle rebuke and said, 'O ye of little faith' (Matthew 6:30, 8:26, 14:31, 16:8). He continually encouraged those who followed him to launch out in faith. He challenged Peter to let down the fishing net after a night of fruitless toil. He commanded the disciples to give the vast multitude food to eat. The results were staggering.

It is important for us to realise, of course, that our faith is based upon fact and not on blind hope. Hebrews 11:1 gives us a definition of faith: 'Now faith is the substance of things hoped for, the evidence of things not seen.' The Greek word for 'substance' means 'a foundation' or a prop on which something can stand and be supported. Our faith is centred in the Almighty himself, of whom it is said, 'God . . . cannot lie.'

The reason why a lot of us are in a state of confusion and despair is that we have trusted in our own philosophies, ideologies and systems. As long as we leave Christ out of our lives, we can expect to go on groping in the dark and being a victim of circumstances. But how different it can be! Each one of us may come to the place where we can say, like Paul, 'I can do all things through Christ which strengtheneth me.' Faith is spoken of in Scripture as 'believing,' 'being persuaded,' 'taking hold,' 'embracing,' and so on. Unless we are prepared to come the biblical way, we shall never experience the triumphant faith of which the Bible speaks. It cannot be conjured up or manufactured by men. As the Apostle Paul points in Ephesians 2:8, faith is not of ourselves, it is 'the gift of God'.

It is tragic that most of us spend our time doubting and limiting God instead of asking him to give us faith that we might go forward with confidence to meet every situation. He is the God of the impossible. The startling and sensational words of Jesus in Matthew 17:20 have been, to a large extent, ignored by the Church, conveniently shelved or interpreted to mean something different from what was actually intended by Christ. We should ponder these golden words and let them put fresh hope into our hearts: 'If ye have faith as a grain of mustard seed, ye shall say unto this mountain, Remove hence to yonder place; and it shall remove; and nothing shall be impossible unto you.'

There is no limit then to what God can do for those who practice his laws of faith. But his blessing depends precisely on the degree to which you believe. Dr W. Sangster said, 'faith is like the sluice gates on a canal or river. You move the great wheel and the gates move a little, and a small trickle of water seeps through . . . Turn the wheel full course and the flood gates open to their widest . . . and you have a flood of power and blessing.'

It is a false concept, a slander against human nature and against God's purposes, that we need be nothing all our lives. God who created us can re-create us! Peter said, you 'were not a people, but are now the people of God . . . had not obtained mercy, but now have obtained mercy.' You were nothing, but God has made you great!

A little negro boy was being laughed at and called names. He had given himself to God, so he prayed to the Lord, then he made a big banner and tied it across the full length of his bedroom, to remind him of the truth. It said, 'I'm me, I'm good, because God doesn't make junk.' He got the message.

In Christ we are kings he is our Lord, and by faith the powers of heaven are unlocked to us. So do not waste time deprecating yourself, your gifts, your blessings, or complaining about your situation or about other people's treatment of you. If your mental slant is tinged with failure thinking and doubt, then mistrust of God's care failure and defeat will follow. Faith is made inoperative by such attitudes.

The old rhyme goes:

If you think you are beaten, you are;
If you think you dare not, you don't;
If you want to win but think you can't

It's almost a cinch, you won't.
If you think you'll lose, your're lost . . .
Life's battles don't always go
To the stronger and faster man,
But sooner or later, the man who wins
Is the man who *thinks he can*.

Cliff Richard's favourite text is, 'I can do all things through Christ which strengtheneth me.' It is a statement of God's spiritual law: when you believe and are in harmony with Jesus, you can handle any situation that confronts you. Emerson said, 'No accomplishment, no assistance, no training can compensate for lack of belief.' Faith is not just to receive what we wants—health, plenty, prosperity, gadgets, or our own desires. It must be built on holiness and obedience, resulting in personal victory, a spiritually sweet disposition, love, joy and peace, and a right relationship and kind attitude to others. These are as much the mark of men and women of biblical faith as receiving all the things we need and desire.

A little sparrow was perched on the edge of a bird bath in the park. Other birds had taken their bath and flown off, but he remained hesitant. Two or three women stood watching.

'What's the matter with the poor little thing?' one asked.

Another commented, 'Let me pick him up and take him home and give him some warmth, he seems ill.'

Then a man who had been watching nearby stepped in 'Let him alone, don't destroy his self-confidence,' he said. 'I have watched him carefully for some time, he is just getting a start in life, leave him alone.'

It became very interesting, and the bystanders stood in silence watching for some minutes. Then the sparrow got enough courage to fly a few feet. The mother and father birds came round and encouraged him, soon a small group of birds gathered, perhaps his relatives, and all chirped and flew around. Soon he was flying up off the birdbath into the air with all the other birds flying alongside him. Those watching marvelled at his spirit, perseverance and final confidence.

Just as with that bird, perseverance, faith, trial and effort, dedication, rejection of negative thoughts, are all vital to victory, and an inflow of divine power. Reject all that blocks the flow of that power. Our failure is not being willing enough to practise the power of faith. We fail to unlock our faith power.

The headmaster of a fine Christian school in London spoke recently about how this splendid school was brought into being from unpromising beginnings. 'I think the banks in our area had their doubts. They felt at times like writing us off. But when I needed finance, God met my needs, and the bank helped too, but with reservations . . . I believe in God's law of supply and demand . . . that he never fails. I just kept on believing this big task had to be done and that faith in the Father would bring this work through . . .'

Any human being can do more with his life with God's help than he is presently doing. Faith is the key. Faith will possess the land, for this is the generation who have come through the wilderness of doubt, and will enter the Land flowing with milk, honey and grapes. The people who unlock their faith power will cross Jordan, bringing down the walls of Jericho AND TAKE OVER THE WHOLE LAND FOR KING JESUS.

VIII: *Get to know what love is!*

Someone has said that the religion of the world today is the pursuit of love. Yet how many of us, I wonder, really understand and practise it. People cry out for love. The music charts have been full of titles such as 'All I need is love,' 'I can't live in a world without love,' 'The glory of love,' 'Love can make the poorest man a millionaire,' 'Love makes the world go round.' Love films have drawn vast audiences, and romance books have had a revival the last few years with Catherine Cookson and Barbara Cartland still top sellers.

I was on a train travelling to a Mission of a few years age, and noticed a man sitting on the opposite side of the carriage with a paperback he was devouring. He was bald headed and must have been in his 60s. I peered round the front of the book and noted the title he was lapping up – it was the romance *Roses Will Never Fade!* When Christianity was born two thousand years age the word 'love' then meant 'lust'. All kinds of perverted sexual practices were indulged in, even by men of eminence. It was so bad that in some areas Aristotle reports that there was a law encouraging unnatural love. At the time of the birth of the Church, moral depravity was eating the heart out of the Roman Empire. This occurred under the guise of love.

Today, the same connotation is being put on this word. The idea has blossomed again through the corrupt imaginations of novelists, playwrights and the like. They advocate a dark, loathsome counterfeit of love.

We have confused this word with uncontrolled passion and eroticism. We see young people in our cities parading the streets unashamedly displaying badges on their garments with slogans like 'Love me' and 'Freedom to fornicate'. No doubt these disillusioned folk are the products of the advocates of the so-called 'free love' doctrine. Evidently these young libertines, many of whom have had university training, are neither mature nor intelligent enough to understand that while sex is closely related to love, it is not love itself. When will these folk grow up to realise that man cannot live by sex alone? True fulfilment doesn't come that way. The whole of history makes this clear.

This is where the Word of God can give guidance that is badly needed today on matters of importance to us all. There are those who declare that Christianity is not relevant and has nothing meaningful to say to this age on these vital subjects. Those who make such statements are either ignorant of what the Bible teaches or are deliberatley ignoring what it has to say.

For instance, the Bible does not condemn sex, as many seem to think that it does. As a matter of fact, the Bible brings it right out into the open and then states quite clearly the best way in which sex should be practised to bring ecstasy and ennoblement to our lives and to build a sound society. The Scriptures teach us that love cannot be complete without sex, but also that sex is not the sum total of it. It has to be the servant of love and not its master. Unless this happens, men and women will be reduced to the level of animals in the field. We all want to be loved. We all need to be loved. Sigmund Freud stated that 'Love is the first requirement of mental health'. As I have prayed for multitudes of people who are depressed, disturbed, or suffering anxiety neuroses, I have often noticed that the doctor's or psychologist's report will say, 'Lacks love' or 'wants to be loved'. *God offers the only stable, healthy, permanent, divine, selfless love.*

A father and young son were on top of a hill viewing the magnificent English country side on a clear summer's day. They could view some seven counties, with green fields, winding river, beautiful trees, little country roads, as far as one could see. The man said to his son, 'Look at that, son, and remember God's love is as vast as all that.' As they gazed all around them from the highest spot in the West of England, the lad

110

said, 'Then we must be right in the middle of God's love!'

The greatest security in my life next to faith, is love. The love of the Father is the backbone to spiritual faith.

At a funeral service on the windswept hillside of Goose Green, as 17 British paras were laid to rest after fierce onslaught during the Falklands conflict, the Padre spoke of one man who ran into the line of fire to defend a friend, facing heavy machine-gun fire. He quoted the words of Jesus: 'Greater love hath no man than this, that a man lay down his life for his friends.' Jesus showed his eternal love for us in giving his life, not only for his friends, but for those of us who were hostile and even his enemies. We are right in the middle of his love for us daily, if we could but realise it. Love in the Church, in the world, in your home, in your heart, makes a difference to the whole of life. W.T.H. Richards used to say that the scourge of the Church for two thousand years has been 'lack of love'. The pastor of a church in Argentina laboured hard and his group grew to 600. Then a word from the Lord came that they were not growing, just getting fat! They asked, 'What do you mean, Lord? He answered, 'Well, first you had 100 people who did not love each other, now you have 600 folk who do love each other. That's not growth, only getting fat.'

'Let us love one another' was the injunction of John. Go out of your way to speak to awkward people, to those you naturally clash with. Be natural, be at ease, learn to show kindness and love to those who do not like you! Send a box of chocs, run an errand, arrange for them to come round for a meal. Show love!

No matter if we are up or down, in difficulties, or in good times, surrounded by friends or opponents, love is the hallmark of life, and love will add the zip that we need.

'In this was manifested the love of God toward us, that God sent his only begotten Son into the world, that we might live through him (1 John 4:9)

'All the religions of the world are men reaching to God,' commented Billy Graham. 'Christianity is different. It is a God of love reaching to men.' A gipsy could not believe God loved him, and a Christian was trying to explain how much God cared for him. The old gipsy said, 'Show me in black and white God loves me and I will believe it.'

The Christian lifted his Bible, turned to the text John 3:16, and showed him the printed text, saying, 'There we have it, in black and white. God so loved the world that he gave his only begotten Son, that whosoever believeth in him should not perish, but have everlasting life.'

Love is the supreme and dominant attitude of God. God said in Jeremiah 31:3, 'I have loved thee with an everlasting love . . . with loving kindness have I drawn thee.' The Bible is a revelation of that love. When I speak of justice, I speak of a justice tempered with love. When I speak of righteousness, I speak of a righteousness founded on love. The atonement is an atonement planned by love, provided by love, given by love, finished by love, necessitated by love. When I speak of the Resurrection, I speak of a miracle of love, and the return of Christ is the final fulfilment of love.

Love makes a mark on a home, on an individual, that never dies away. *Love is life*.

In Paul's first letter to the Corinthians (13:4–7) we find the greatest exposition of love that has ever been written. We are given positive and negative pictures. We are told that love which builds strong character and makes for harmony and progress knows how to exercise control and is temperate in all things. Love is not bigoted, selfish, suspicious or envious. It is not arrogant nor conceited. It does not cherish inflated ideas of its own self importance. It has no time for shady dealings or iniquitous practices. True love, says the Apostle, can be trusted, it is patient and courteous to others. It is liberal, humble, cheerful and always concerned about the welfare of others, and it never gives up hope that the most depraved person will make good. It stands always for truth and is kind to all. Love delights to give to another for his or her happiness an in so doing finds its own fulfilment.

Men mock at these virtues today and people who propagate them are ridiculed as being old-fashioned and insipid. But the fact remains that they have been tested and their worth has been proved. We see them perfectly blended in the character of the man Christ Jesus.

What we often fail to realise is that worthwhile service is always motivated by love, and those who profess to be Christian disciples should remember this, if they desire to go forth to help others in the spirit of their Master. It is true that the Son of God promised to give his followers the power of the Holy Spirit to enable them to face all kinds of opposition and triumph, but he made it quite clear that love was to be the spring of their actions. Paul, the great pioneer of the New Testament, exemplified this and could write in 2 Corinthians 5:14, '*The love of Christ constrains [controls] us*'. It is when we are mastered by this love that we become effective Christians. Then the Christian Gospel will have an impact on those outside the fold. Gandhi made this point clear when he said, '*If you come to us in the spirit of Jesus Christ, we will not be able to resist you.*' In the words of Irene Taylor of Lossiemouth:

Why do I love you?
Why are you so fragrant?
Why does your smile light up my day?
Why do you return all the love I feel?
Why do you care? You walk Jesus' way.

I often think of the story which the great Buckinghamshire preacher W.T.H. Richards once told me, when discussing love. He said, 'Invariably two young men come to my mind, both of whom were friends of mine. They died at about the same age of 27 years and of the same complaint, tuberculosis. One lived in Wales and the other in England. Their deaths occurred about 35 years apart, but they had one thing in common. Almost with their dying breath they spoke of the subject of love. The one gasped out a prayer, 'Lord give Thy people more love.' The other, who had prayed for healing, said to his loved one, 'Mother, whether God heals me or not, I will love him just the same.' In the first there was a request for a manifestation of true love by Christians. God knows how much that is needed today. The other was a demonstration of it!'

It would be good for us to keep before us always the noble reply Jesus gave to the young lawyer who asked what was the greatest commandment. Jesus answered, 'Thou shalt love the lord thy God with all thy heart, and with all thy soul, and with all thy mind, and with all thy strength: this is the first commandment. And the second is like, namely this, Thou shalt love thy neighbour as thyself.' This is the very heart of the Christian message. The Bible tells in unmistakable language, by precept and practice, that the only way to build a better world is by manifesting supreme love to God and unselfish love to our neighbour.

Christ is the source of all true deep love. The story goes of the restaurateur the late Emil Mettler, remembered so well not only for his high standards and kind words, but for his generous loving actions. One day a man stood near the cash register, and when Emil took out his change, the man was astonished to see a six inch nail in the till. He asked what it was for. Emil replied that he always kept that there, so that as he thought of how much he was prospering, it would remind him of the one who paid such a price for him and his salvation—Jesus Christ. 'I remember the extent of his love,' Emil put it, 'and what I owe him in return in my love and devotion.' No wonder he was missed so much!

An ex-wrestler was one day joking with some friends. He had been a great champion, but he surprised them by boasting, 'I could get out of any hold my opponent put on me.' His friends doubted this, even for such an expert. Then he clarified it: 'I could get out, because all I would have to do is GIVE IN AND THE REFEREE would break the hold . . .'! They all roared with laughter—it was the easy way out!

To experience God's love and power, and to be able to manifest it, demands a similar surrender, and costs all we are. But when we do 'GIVE IN' to the love of God, we break the 'hold' of our opponents—carnality, evil, temptation, weakness, compromise, fruitlessness, defeatism, depression, fear, frustration. They are all released as we move into the covering and empowering of God's love.

IX: *Family Harmony*

Can a person truly have life who does not have harmony in home and family? Dr William Barclay commented, 'Life without home is the bleakest prospect I can conceive . . .' I believe tranquillity, joy and happiness in family life is vital to healthy, balanced and contented living. God reminded the people in the time of Micah, 'I sent before thee Moses, Aaron, and Miriam' (Micah 6:4). God pointed out that their amazing escape from Egypt was due to this remarkable family. Of course in so many ways they were all different. Moses was a prophet, Aaron a High Priest, Miriam a prophetess. They supplied all the leadership this vast group of people needed in their wilderness journey, Moses with the precepts to guide, Aaron with the prayers to gladden, Miriam with the praises to glorify God.

God has used families ever since, and has blessed home life with contentment, unity and harmony.

The first marriage was in the Garden of Eden, where God instituted the union of man and wife. In Genesis 2:18 we read, 'And the Lord God said, It is not good that the man should be alone; I will make him an help meet for him'. One of the first great love stories is of Isaac, who 'took Rebecca and she became his wife, and he loved her'.

Before the Church, the government or school, the home was founded – it is the *basic unit of society*!

'God setteth the solitary in families' (Psalm 68:6) – he invented the family structure. The early Church is the supreme example of happy, harmonious living in families. In the apostolic band, our Lord chose three sets of brothers: Peter and Andrew, James and John, and Matthew and his twin brother, Thomas. Two of our Lord's brothers held prominent positions in the

Jerusalem church – James, bishop of that city, and Jude, who composed a fiery terse Epistle. Then also, later, there were Aquila and Priscilla, Andronicus and Junia, and Tryphena and Tryphosa, who were probably twin sisters.

Philip the evangelist did not neglect his family. He had four daughters at home who prophesied! Timothy is reminded about his good family background – of 'thy grandmother Lois', whose faith he shared.

Down through history this has been repeated in many other *lovely partnerships*. Samuel and Susanah Wesley raised 17 children, amongst them the three great brothers, John, Charles and the lesser-known evangelist Samuel (named after his father), who between them shaped the spiritual and family life of Britain and influenced it for good, for 100 years! Look at the Booth family in the nineteenth century, used of God to establish the great social, philanthropic and evangelical work, the Salvation Army. William had six children, all of whom became evangelists! Look at the Jeffereys family from South Wales – George, Stephen, William, and one of the sons, Edward, who shook Britain with their great evangelistic endeavours before the last war. A family that brought healing to thousands of sick people, and touched the heart of the nation with their love and compassion.

What is the secret? Behind Moses, Miriam and Aaron was the faith of their parents, Jochebed and Amram, who were of such spiritual quality that they gained a place in the gallery of the heroes of faith in Hebrews 11:23! How important to family life is *mother*! When Napoleon was asked what France needed more than anything else, he replied: 'GOOD MOTHERS'! Old Billy Sunday, the evangelist, used to say, 'If you want to beat the devil, knock him over the head with a cradle.'

I shall never forget an old lady I stayed with in New York State, USA, in 1971 when on a preaching tour. She was in her seventies then. Her husband had died way back in the 1930s during the Depression, just after she had given birth to her sixth child. She had no paid work, no dole money, and six children to feed. She worked on her little farm with horses and cart, grew the wheat, fed, clothed and brought up her family with no mod-cons like washing machines, dishwashers, vacuum cleaners, electric irons, fridges, or freezers. She did it all alone! I asked her, 'How did you do it?'

She replied, 'I prayed for two hours every day.'

Amazing! A woman with no husband, no money, no gadgets, no car, working hard to provide for and bring up six children, and yet she was content, satisfied and happy, for she found time through all those years to pray for two hours every afternoon without fail.

I asked her about her children. They had all done well in life. Three were ministers in the Church, two of the girls were married to ministers and serving God, the sixth was doing well in business and was a member of his local church. Radiant successful living in family life indeed!

Campbell Morgan had four sons who all became ministers. At a family reunion, a friend asked, 'Which of you Morgans is the best preacher?' The eldest son replied: 'Mother!'

John Wesley told how he 'learned more of Christianity from my Mother than all the theologians of England.'

Many great men have testified to the lasting impact of good contented family life centred on a devoted mother: St Bernard, the noted writer Dodridge, Walter Scott the poet, and evangelists like Oral Roberts and Billy Graham, among many others. I give testimony to the wonderful influence of a marvellous mother in my own life.

Great artists have put their mothers into oil paintings which become priceless, they so respected and honoured them – like Rubens, Titian the great Italian painter, and Joshua Reynolds the English landscape painter.

At the other end of the spectrum, we see the hideous results of a bad mother on home life and children's upbringing, and consequently their evil impact in history. For instance Nero had a drunken mother, and the great poet who died at a young age in such despair, Lord Byron, had a proud and violent mother.

The famous child actress, Judy Garland, had a mum who, it is alleged was unfaithful to Judy's father. This caused Judy to hate and despise her mother, in the end leading her to barbiturates and a sudden death.

If you are married, what are the precepts for making marriage work with supreme satisfaction and success? The ceremony is over; the honeymoon is past; what are the vital rules to observe? I call these the four 'A's for a happy marriage:

1. *Learn to accept.* You cannot know a person until you live with them. Idiosyncrasies will surface, peculiarities appear, temperamental differences become evident – but now that you have chosen your spouse, accept all that this choice involves. Hurtful attempts to bend your partner to your own whims and ways can be destructive. It is often wiser to accept the inevitable – like Jacob did when he lifted Leah's veil and found that she was not what he thought!

2. *Learn to adapt.* No longer can you go your own way, you are in a new partnership: 'heirs together of the grace of life' (1 Peter 3:7). This applies not only biologically, but also psychologically: you not only sleep together, you live together. Not only will there be a discovery of unsuspected qualities in each other, there should also be an acknowledgement of them. Be grateful for each other's graces. And those kindly touches! Never cease to be courteous: always be ready to say 'thank you' (yes, and 'sorry' too, when necessary). Those marriages last where courtship never ceases.

Here are a few guidelines for husbands:

1. Understand your wife and look out for her welfare.
2. Keep the channels of communication open and clear.
3. Set an example.
4. Make sound and timely decisions.
5. Encourage your wife's capabilities.
6. Seek responsibility and take it.

Men should take note that the Anglo-Saxon word for 'husband' means 'the band of the house', the one who binds it together, supplies for it, organises it, controls it, and holds it in unity! I urge you to show politeness to the one who walks by your side through the years.

And for the wife – ask yourself these pertinent questions:

1. 'I vowed to love and to cherish' – have I begun to take him for granted?
2. 'In sickness and in health' – Do I complain when sickness comes and shakes the rigid plan of everyday life?
3. 'For better or for worse' – Is it really for worse—When he doesn't fit in with all my ideas and wants, all the time?
4. 'Forsaking all other' – Am I absolute in my fidelity and faithfulness?

Ogden Nash, a modern day writer, offered succinct advice when he wrote:

> To keep your marriage brimming
> With love in the loving cup
> When you're wrong admit it
> When you're right shut up

3. *Learn to associate*. I remember Cliff Barrows' motto for marriage: 'Marriages are held together by twelve words – I'm wrong! I'm sorry! Please forgive me! I love you!'

Mrs Billy Graham, asked what made a successful married couple, replied, 'Two good forgivers.' It is also vital to do things together: go out together, spend time on golfing, picnicking, visiting places, shopping (even if, like me, you find it very boring, struggling around from shop to shop for hours!). The new saying is true: 'The family that plays together stays together.'

Above all try to go to the same church; share your spiritual life together. Pray together and then you *will* stay together!

When the husband or wife is under pressure, with doubts or trials, (or when ministers are under special attack), hide yourself away with your partner, cling together, agonise together, support each other securely till you are through the storm.

Do be considerate, husbands. I know you are busy building a home, supplying a home, caring for your loved one and children, but do not lose your wife and home by putting too much energy into supplying for them.

Marriage means sharing. While each has separate duties, there should always be mutual interest, concern and care. Pull together, or you may be pulled apart. True marriage is like a reef knot, which tightens with the strain.

4. *Learn to be affectionate.* Love can die; bitterness takes its place. 'Husbands, be sure you give your wife much love and sympathy; don't let bitterness or resentment spoil your marriage' (Colossians 3:19, Phillips). Share the same interests, the same outlook, the same friends: don't live separate lives. Let your feelings be made gentle by a touch of the Spirit of God. Paul speaks of the place of 'prayer and fasting' in the context of married life (I Corinthians 7:5), and Peter talks of an atmosphere of understanding and of tenderness in which prayer may carry on unhindered (Peter 3:7).

A marriage counsellor made a remarkable observation, that she had never counselled a Christian couple who prayed together regularly, but had interviewed many who said they used to!

Aaron Linford expressed it in these words: 'Seek each other's welfare that love may grow and flourish. True love 'seeketh not her own', if husband and wife love each other (in the highest sense). But let it not be a onesided affair. Marriage is being 'yoked together' in a yoke—the two so harnessed, that they must pull together in the same direction and with the same fervour . . .'

The Word of God says, 'Husbands, love your wives' – this is a divine injunction. But why are not wives told to love in return? Is it that women so readily respond to affection that they do not need this exhortation? As Lord Byron said:

Man's love is of man's life a thing apart;
'Tis woman's whole existence.

Married love must be mutual to be perfected. But what does this term 'love' imply? Not merely physical gratification – that could descend to lust – but a oneness of heart.

Edna St Vincent Millay reminded us in her poem:

'Tis not love's going that hurts my days,
But that it went *in little ways* . . .

Don't let your love life slowly dry up, keep it alive, watch it, keep it burning.

A theologian paraphased 1 Corinthians 13:4–7 in words which are ideal for marriage: 'Such love is patient and gentle, is not jealous, does not show off or have inflated ideas of its own importance, is not rude, is unselfish, sweet-tempered, not suspicious. It knows no malice, is always ready to commend what is good; it is understanding, trustful, optimistic and steadfast.' Isn't that what true love is all about?

Peter exhorts that husbands should deal graciously with their wives, 'as unto the weaker vessel' (1 Peter 3:7). Not weaker in moral virtues, or in mental capacity, but (generally speaking) in physical strength. More than that, the psychological make-up of a woman calls for gentler dealing: a woman is special creation of God. As Aaron Linford put it, she is as 'delicate as a porcelain, mysterious as the sphinx and as sensitive as a passion flower.' But it works both ways, for how powerful can be the submission of a wife to her husband.

The Scriptures encourage women to accept a place of submission: 'Wives, submit yourselves unto your own husbands, as unto the Lord, for the husband is the head of the wife . . .[being] obedient to their own husbands . . . ye wives, be in subjection to your own husbands' (Ephesians 5:22-23, Titus 2:5, 1 Peter 3:1). Someone said to me, 'Yes, the man is the head, but the woman is the neck that turns the head!' This does not not mean dogmatic, arrogant, brutal, chauvinistic dictatorship by the man, but that he is a *slightly* ahead of the woman in having to maintain, showing the lead, meeting her need and supporting her.

Finally the three 'S's which lead to a satisfying marriage relationship.

1. *Self control*. This word comes from a Greek term meaning 'Strong' or 'able to control one's thoughts and actions'. Having a mind in control – this is vital to good marriages. We all err here and make our blunders, but the sooner we mature and learn this lesson, the happier family relationship will be. Susannah Wesley wrote to her sons, John and Charles, when they were at Oxford and warned them: 'Anything which increases the authority of the body over the mind is an evil.' Be in control of your emotions, your personal life, your home.

The Christian virtue of self-control is as essential for domestic harmony as in other spheres of life. This applies to temper. Free minds will sometimes differ; a slave-mentality is no sure basis for married bliss. Nevertheless, brakes should be put on any dispute when it is approaching the borders of passion. Don't work out your frustrations on your family. It also applies to temperament. While I cannot be other than myself, yet I must seek those adjustments that make cohabitation a joy and not a pain. Then what of time? Married life should be so controlled that there is time to pray together, to have recreation together, to enjoy family life together.

Mark Twain's poem called 'A Marriage' sums it up:

A marriage makes of two fractional lives a whole,
it gives two purposeless lives a work,
and doubles the strength of each to perform it.
It gives to two questioning natures –
a reason for being, and something to live for.
It will give a new gladness to the sunshine,
and new fragrance to the flowers,
and new beauty to the earth,
and a new mystery to life.

Also, of course, responsibilities should be shouldered together, chores shared and joint-duties accepted. While there may be 'man-jobs' and 'woman-jobs', the workload should be spread by an equal distributions of onus and mutual agreement of work allotment, whether by tacit consent or after discussion. While due consideration should be given to relative strength, ability and opportunity, no wife should have to do it all and no husband should be burdened with a double load. God created Eve to be a 'help' for the man she is joined to in wedlock.

2. *A sacred covenant.* Do you remember those vows you made when you 'plighted your troth' together? 'For richer, for poorer; in sickness and in health; to love and to cherish, till death us do part.' You meant them at the time but how different they appear in the context of everyday life! Let this sacred covenant be an anchor to your affections in turbulent times. Hold them fast through life's vicissitudes. You belong to him whose vows you received: he belongs to you. Job refused to let his eyes stray to another woman (Job 31:1); he was a covenanted man. He wore the blinkers of love (and duty) that had eyes for only one woman – the woman he had married.

Marriage is for life. Today when troubles come to a home, often young people turn to divorce, which is now so easy to obtain. When Jesus asked, 'Is it lawful for a man to put away his wife?' he replied, 'What therefore God has joined together, let not man put asunder' (Matthew 19:3,6). Paul wrote in Romans 7:2, 'The woman which hath an husband is bound by the law to her husband *as long as he liveth.*'

Today marriage is mocked; cohabitation without the sanctity of grace or the sanction of law is common; wife-swapping is regarded as a joke; divorce – now involving more than one in three marriages – is rampant. What can Christians do to counter this 'corruption that is in the world through lust'?

One great contribution we can make is to show that marriage works. If we can prove that God's ideal of one-man-one-woman relationship 'until death do us part' is not only endurable but also enjoyable, we shall be acting as 'the salt of the earth' and help preserve society from moral putrefaction.

But Christians, too, have problems. How may we face the pressures of life in a permissive environment, and at the same time maintain a happy home? Subject to a thousand stresses and strains in the climate of a 'do-as-you-like' philosophy, can we resist the pull of contempory society? By God's *grace and power* we can.

William Shakespeare reminded us of the solidness of 'true love' in his great poem of that name . . .

Love is not, love
Which alters when it alteration finds . . .
O, no! it is an ever-fixed mark,
That looks on tempests and is never shaken . . .
Love alters not with his brief hours and weeks,
but bears it out even to the edge of doom . . .

Some years ago my eldest boy was small, travelling with us from town to town as we pioneered different churches and held many campaigns, a lady said to him, 'How sad you do not have a settled home.'

He replied very indignantly, 'We have a home, but not a house to fit it into!'

He knew that where there was love, there was home. Home is not bricks and mortar, material possessions, toys, gadgets and trinklets – but a unity, a peace, a love, a security!

Judge Joseph Sabath has had long and varied experience with the legal aspects of broken homes and wrecked marriages. He has presided for twenty years over what he calls 'the nightmare world of the divorce courts'. He says, 'Ninety thousand people, who have come to the parting of the ways through bitter recriminations, have stood before me to testify of broken homes, sordid betrayals, and the unbelievable rancour which causes separations . . . Out of my fifty years of married life, and my twenty years as a divorce judge, I have framed a decalogue for those who are married or who are contemplating it which I think could prevent at least 90 per cent of the marital smash-ups. Here from me are the rules of a successful marriage:

1. Bear and forbear.
2. Work together, play together and grow up together.
3. Avoid the little quarrels and the big ones will take care of themselves.
4. Compromise (give and take). It is the antitoxin of divorce.
5. Practise sympathy, good humour and mutual understanding.
6. Don't grumble before breakfast or after it.
7. Respect your "in-laws", but don't criticise them or take criticism from them.
8. Establish your own home, even in a one-room flat.
9. Fight for each other, but not with each other.
10. Build your home on religious faith, with love and forgiveness as the watchwords.'

Browning said, 'A happy home is an early heaven'. The expression is used 5 times in the Bible, and there are no less than twelve different Greek words to cover it. The most common is *oikos* – 'one's proper home'.

A true home is built on God's love and power, and solid statistics support this. For instance in a survey some years ago by the Bureau of Census in the USA, it was found that out of regular church attenders only one in 57 marriages ended with divorce; out of the homes where both read the Bible and pray together with daily family prayers, only one in 500 homes ended in divorce. But on the other hand, where families did neither, 55 in 100 ended in the divorce courts! This shows clearly that the Bible's strong family concept and spiritual teaching on this matter are relevant today, and are the only practical answer to save family life. The old adage is still true – 'the family that prays together, stays together'. May we make Christ the centre of our homes, and build them to the glory of God.

3. Finally we have *the salvation of marriage*. Gipsy Smith used to say, 'The home without Christ in it, is like a room without a fire or heating in it on a winter's day

– empty, uninviting and cold.' May we make Christ the centre of our homes and build them on his Word, his faith, his strength and his values.

Look at your life, and ask yourself:

Is TV more important than the Bible?
Is entertainment more important than prayer?
Is pleasure-seeking more important than principles?
Is accumulating money more important than time with family?
Are worldly possessions more important than a loving partnership?

If the answer is yes, you have much trouble ahead in your marriage. Let the Lord take first place in your married life. Honour his Word, submit to his will, engage in his service, seek his face in prayer, not only in times of crisis but in regular worship. And remember, if tempers have flared, irritations become evident, a hint of boredom is seen, cling even closer to God and one another. For as it says in Ecclesiastes 4:9-12, 'Two are better than one . . . For if they fall, the one will lift up his fellow . . . Again if two lie together, then they have heat . . . And if one prevail against him, two shall withstand him; and a three-fold cord is not quickly broken.' We produce more work, we hold one another up, we cheer each other along, we fight life's battles together. What a picture of marital blessings!

But note the great encouragement in the final word here – 'and a threefold cord is not quickly broken.' When God comes into the married situation – a heavenly third party – the matrimonial bond is strengthened against all stress and strain. This plaited union is unbreakable! Such a home provides the secure basis which is vital in the ongoing experience of abundant living.

X: *Watch those small things*

When the *Titanic* struck an iceberg on her maiden voyage in April 1912, James Kruch of Chicago, Illinois, was on board. After a harrowing ordeal he was eventually rescued. Then when German submarines torpedoed the *Lusitania* on 7 May 1915, Kruch was again on board a doomed ship. For the second time he was rescued.

But years later, when he was crossing a shallow stream. Kruch collapsed and drowned. This man, who had survived twice in the ocean, lost his life in less than one foot of water!

Berkeley was an explorer, mountain climber and big game hunter. He had shot lions and tigers and other dangerous animals, chalking up quite a record for himself. Then he was killed, not by the claws of a charging lion or the cunning stealth of a man-eating tiger, but by the scratch of a barnyard cat! Blood poisoning set in and killed him.

Blondin made crowds gasp when he walked over the Niagara Falls on a tightrope. Few feats of daring had been seen to compare to it. He was hailed as the 'Conqueror of Niagara'. Then Blondin died in Ealing, London, on 19 February 1897. His death was hastened by his tripping over a doormat outside his own house!

Little things destroy life.

The wife of a former minister wept as she told me between sobs of her husband's infidelity. He now had to leave the manse, his salary had been suspended, a good faithful ministry of nearly 40 years was over, his good name was ruined and the world treated him with ridicule. She grieved that after years of faithfulness she was left alone, broken, in despair.

The 40-year-old former businessman, immaculately dressed in Burberry coat, Cambridge suit and Van

Heusen white shirt, shook nervously, his hand literally shuddering, as he recounted his story. Fantastic business deals, large amounts of money, rapid wealth, a meteoric rise in the City and business world—then suddenly it came crashing down, his friends lost, his family about to break up, his bank account overdrawn.

The young housewife was more philosophical and had dried her tears, but the shock to her system was just as deadly. Her husband had been doing so well as a policeman, with promotion in prospect. Then seemingly innocently he picked up a 12-year-old girl on a wet afternoon, dropped her off where she requested, and at the last moment either by design or by a sheer accident put his hand on her knee. She screamed and jumped from the car, took his number and reported it to the authorities. It meant a court case, a guilty verdict, loss of job and home. How can I trust him again? this young wife murmured.

These stories I have heard and similar cases I have encountered would fill a book on their own, but in all of them, and I would think at least 80 per cent of all cases we have counselled, the tragedy can be traced to a *small first defect*.

In the first case the tragedy of the lonely minister's wife began when he allowed himself to become over-friendly with a young woman who came for counselling. Then in the second case a lack of watchfulness in small financial matters, letting go on tiny principles, led to larger issues. And in the third case, who would have imagined that one day, a general over-friendliness would lead him into either a big mistake, or an innocent momentary error that would destroy him.

Life has been marred for many people by some small issue—a weakness, sin, carelessness, misuse of time, or lack of wisdom.

For Achan it was a wedge of gold, pieces of silver and a garment under the floor – meaning later disgrace and even death.

For Saul a few head of cattle he should have left alone—and his disobedience commenced a string of errors leading him to suicide.

For Samson, a short sleep on Delilah's knee – ending in horrible blindness and degradation.

For Miriam murmuring against her brother Moses – the terrible judgement of leprosy.

Solomon warned about small things that can bring ruin: 'Take us the foxes, the little foxes, that spoil the vines: for our vines have tender grapes.' How safe are your vines, how tender your grapes?

The old verse goes:

For the want of a nail a shoe was lost,
For the want of a horse a rider was lost,
For the want of a rider a battle was lost,
For the want of a battle a kingdom was lost,
And all for the want of a horseshoe nail . . .

Small things are important.

Here are *six small aspects of life* to which we should pay great attention. They are: vision, thanks, speech, awe and wonder, friendships, and self-surrender.

1. *Vision.* Guard against the dimming of vision. Keep to your dreams. As Dr Yonggi Cho said, 'Don't kill your dreams – execute them!'

A young man questioned the ability of God to make any difference in his life. His father produced an apple, cut it in half and took out a seed. Then he asked his son, 'What do you see?'

The boy saw only an apple seed and answered, 'Nothing really, I see nothing.'

His father replied, 'Son, where you see nothing there dwells a mighty tree.'

In the Old Testament there are amazing stories of men and women whom God used to bring about deliverance for his people. Men and women who laid hold of God and accomplished great things in their generation. Two men that stand out are Elijah and Elisha.

1 Kings Chapter 17 records Elijah's appearance almost out of nowhere and he begins to demonstrate some tremendous miracles with the Word of the Lord. The

rain is withheld and the dead are raised.

1 Kings Chapter 19 records the emergence of Elisha who becomes Elijah's servant. 1 Kings Chapter 2 shows Elisha's devotion and service to Elijah, the end result being a double portion of the Spirit of God.

Here we see the passing on of the anointing from one servant to another. Because of Elisha's faithfulness he receives God-given ability to fulfil the purposes of God in his life. God had the right man to fill Elijah's shoes when it was time for him to go.

Now we also discover that Elisha had a servant by the name of Gehazi (2 Kings 4:12). Gehazi was to be Elisha's servant, a man whom I believe Elisha could trust, a man in whom Elisha could impart something of the Spirit of God that he had received through being a servant.

A study of the meaning of these names reveals some very interesting facts. Elijah means My God is Jehovah. Elisha means God is Salvation. Gehazi means Vale of Vision.

I see from this that Gehazi is a follower of Elisha and is destined to take over the vision and direction that God had given to Elisha. God had a plan for Gehazi's life as he has for us, but as we know, we win or lose by the way we choose.

2 Kings Chapter 5 gives us the story of Naaman and his healing by seven duckings in a dirty stream. Naaman wishes to reward Elisha, but the man of God refuses to accept a reward for doing God's will. We see however the opposite reaction in the life of Gehazi who goes for gold. If Elisha doesn't want the reward, he does. This led to subsequent lying and disastrous results, Gehazi becoming a leper.

Here is a man with so much potential, so much ability, even vision as his name implies, tempted to go for gold instead of following after the Lord. The reward that was offered by Namaan was worth approximately £20,000. Little did he know, but Gehazi was selling his place in God for mere gold.

He was tempted, he gave way, and instead of following hard after God, he allowed himself to be distracted. Instead of being a man of vision he ended up in a valley where lepers lived isolated and outcast. *The vale of lost vision.*

We as believers also have great potential in God. But like Gehazi we can also find ourselves in the Vale of Lost Vision if we become distracted by this world.

Temptations seldom break your door down. They quietly and cunningly slip through the open portals of your mind.

Temptations are certain to ring your doorbell but it is your own fault if you ask them to stay for dinner.

Tozer declared 'The greatest problem of the Church is compromise!'

Jesus said in Luke 9:62, 'No man, after putting his hand to the plough, and looking back, is fit for the kingdom of God.'

Billy Sunday used to say, 'If anyone thinks back, and looks back, it isn't long before he goes back.'

Thomas à Kempis wrote in the fifteenth century, 'Many are deceived in the end who at first were led by the Spirit.'

Tozer warned, 'We have been so involved in the work of the Lord, that we have forgotten the Lord of the work.'

'We look not at the things which are seen, for . . . the things which are not seen are eternal' (2 Corinthians 4:18)

Keep to the vision you have. Let your heart be gripped by it. You may find it difficult to live for God, – your background may not be a Christian family, you may go to a church that is anything but healthy. I knew a man who lived amongst a crowd of ungodly people, his parents were divorced, his folk did not love him or want him, his brothers and sisters were immoral, his relatives lived for money and materialism. But he made it—he became a winner for Christ. He had abundant life all his days. I asked him, 'How did you do it?' One of the reasons he gave me was, 'I never lost my vision . . .'

You may have started off with a strong sense of purpose and vision in your life, desiring to serve God and do his will, but due to temptation find yourself visionless, in a valley, wondering why you have no sense of vision.

We should echo the Lord's prayer, 'Lead us not into temptation but deliver us from evil.' We must guard our vision, redirect our sight, lest we also like Gehazi end up in The Vale of Lost Vision.

We must see Christ, recapture the vision of the Cross and Resurrection, be restored to the sparkling purity, optimism, dynamism, vitality and faith-restoring action of the first Christians. Many, I know, have sold out the great vision they had from God for prestige and professional advantage. They have compromised, they have lost their visualising of God's great plan for them. We have lost the vision splendid through cold-heartedness, compromise, fear of others, through spiritual weakness and worldliness.

Recapture the vision of the glorified, exalted, all-powerful, magnificent, almighty God. . . .

- Moses visualised—he 'endured by seeing him who is invisible . . .'
- Gideon visualised – he believed a dream and told the army, 'Arise, for the Lord hath delivered into your hand the host of Midian.'
- Isaiah visualised – 'I saw the Lord, high and lifted up . . .'
- Jesus visualised – 'Look on the fields; for they are white already to harvest.'

The disciples were given the great vision: 'Occupy till I come . . .'

Paul saw a vision, and fell before the Risen Lord on the Damascus Road. Years later near the end of his life, he was able to recount that day and say, 'I was not disobedient unto the heavenly vision . . .'

The God of Abraham, Isaac, Jacob, Peter and John is still with us. *He blesses and prospers men and women who visualise.* The God of Wesley, Whitefield, Billy Bray, Evan Roberts, Smith Wigglesworth, Charles Price and David Wilkinson is still alive and blessing those with a vision!

If we are to visualize and achieve them we must treat our dreams, visions and ideas with the greatest respect. Here is some advice from a great American pastor, who ministers in one of America's largest churches:

> Treat your ideas, visions, dreams tenderly – they can get killed pretty quickly.
> Treat them gently—they can get bruised in infancy.
> Treat them protectively—do not let them get away.
> Treat them nutritionally—feed them, and feed them well
> Treat them antiseptically—don't let them get infected with the germs of doubt or negative thinking.
> Treat them reverently—they could be the most precious things that have ever come into life since you found God!

Jim Williams wrote:
VISUALISE – for every goal is a statement of faith.
VISUALISE – he who aims at nothing is sure to fail.
VISUALISE – I would rather attempt something great and fail than attempt nothing and succeed!

Pray, claim it, assume victory, see it in your mind's eye, write it on your prayer list, soak it in intercession, get God's mind, aim for it, work at it, plan, organise, believe it into being! *Claim territory from Satan, assume victory from God, reach for your goals.* VISUALISE. Go at it, work at it, keep the vision before you. If we have a great vision we can change circumstances, turn tables, bring the unquenchable answer to every dilemma. Will it, work at it, set your mind on it, change things by your VISION.

2. *Thanks*. A little boy was asked by his Mum if he had thanked his hostess when he was leaving the children's party. He said, 'Well no . . . the girl in front of me did and the lady replied, 'Don't mention it' – so I thought I'd better not . . .'!

Ivan Turgenev, the famous Russian novelist, met a ragged beggar. He stopped and the man thought he was going to give him a coin, but Turgenev put his hand in his pocket and found he had no money. So he held out his hand and warmly shook the beggar's cold palm, saying, 'I'm terribly sorry I have nothing to give you . . .' The beggar smiled and replied, 'Never mind, but thank you for this – your handshake is a gift worth having.'

How rich a gift is a thank you, a smile, a kindly thought, good cheer, an encouragement, sympathy, love.

We need to show our gratitude. There is something special about the grateful person. They have a plus in life.

The Bible says, 'Let us come before his presence with thanksgiving.' More than 30 times the Psalmist speaks of giving thanks. He wrote, 'it is a good thing to give thanks unto the Lord'. At the grave of Lazarus, Jesus said, 'Father, I thank thee that thou has heard me . . .' Let us show gratitude.

When I have bowed my head and given thanks for my meal on trains, in cafés and elsewhere, people have commented that they never seen anyone do that before.

One day in a restaurant two men made a wager, when they saw a man enter who had a small cross on his lapel, signifying he had some religious interest. They bet with each other that he would not publicly bow his head and pray before he ate. The Christian did not know anyone was watching. He was a shy person and found it difficult to do such a thing before others, but with great determination he bowed his head. The man who lost the bet went and accosted him afterwards, telling him how brave he thought he was, and through the ensuing conversation the man who lost his bet, found his God!

Travelling through north Lincolnshire towards the largest single span bridge in the world, the famous Humber bridge, I stopped a man who was out walking and asked for directions to the bridge. He remarked first of all how expensive it was to cross it, then gave some lengthy directions, and his last comment was another blurb on how much they charged to go over it. I had to ask another person and he spoke in the same vein. 'Jolly robbery it is, what they charge to go over the thing . . .'

Then I saw it on the horizon. What a sight! As I approached, I drove slowly to take in the breathtaking curve of this the largest and most expensive bridge ever built. It was magnificent. Soon I was the two miles or more over this marvellous structure spanning the great River Humber near Hull, Yorkshire. I had to queue up behind two other cars to pay at the toll gate. I could hear the man in the first car swearing about the cost of crossing to a seemingly indifferent toll collector. Across in the other exit I could see but not hear a red-faced man waving his fist out of the car at the figure in the collecting booth.

Finally it was my turn at the window, which revealed the blank look of the official. I asked him how much and he announced '£1'. There was no 'Sir' or 'please'. He looked fed up.

I leaned across with my money, smiled and said, 'A marvellous feat of engineering this, it's a wonderful bridge to drive over . . .' The attendant looked as if he could not believe what he had heard. I went on, 'It would be cheap at double the price. Thank you for such a marvellous service.'

The official leaned out of his little window, and looked at me as if I was mad! Then he brightened, smiled, at risk of cracking a face muscle and said, 'Thank you, Sir, it's nice to be appreciated.' With another thank you and a wave I headed north to the Bible Week I was going to preach at. There is joy, power and release in gratitude.

The Bible is a thanksgiving book. Many great men were grateful for what they had been blessed with. The priests gave thanks, part of the Law of Moses was to give thanks, Miriam danced and gave thanks, the Psalms urged, 'Oh give thanks unto the Lord for he is good.' There is something satisfying in saying 'thank you'.

In an old legend a farmer sent his three sons up a mountain to see what they could find. One came back with a bunch of flowers, the second with some beautiful stones. The third came back with nothing, but said, 'I climbed to the top, Father, there was nothing but bare rock. But, Father, I saw the sea afar off, it was

magnificent. I am just so thankful to our Creator!'
The others brought back something in their hands,
he brought back *something in his heart* – thankfulness!
An ancient abbey, a stone and thatched cottage in the
Wiltshire vales, a lovely forest like the Savernake near
my home, a work of art, a great orchestra, a stately
home – how rich they can make us, how thankful we
should be.

Paul repeatedly encouraged us to 'cease not to give
thanks . . . giving thanks for all things . . . abounding
with thanksgiving . . . we are bound to give thanks
always.'

The young man had become increasingly exasperated
as he stood at the shop door, holding it open for the
steady stream of people who passed through without a
word of thanks.

Unable to contain himself any longer, he called
after the last entrant, 'Don't say thank you, it's habit
forming!'

We seem to have lost the art or habit of observing
simple courtesies, even the simplest custom of saying
thank you. Without doubt we are the poorer for it.

A prayer in the Service Book of the Church of England makes us confess, 'We have taken great benefits
with little thanks', and that seems to be so true in our
contemporary world.

Ambrose of Milan said, 'No duty is more urgent than
the returning of thanks.' In Shakespeare's King Henry
VI, part 2, the Duke of Suffolk declares: 'Oh Lord, that
lends me life, lend me a heart replete with thankfulness.'

When William Temple was Archbishop of Canter-
bury he used an illustration that many people have
quoted since. 'This world,' he said, 'is like a shop
window into which someone mischievous has crept
and switched around the price-tags. Those things which
were dear have become cheap, and the cheap things
grossly inflated in price.' Courtesy is regarded as of little
value, and the expression of thanks with indifference.

Add to this the question of example. We are still creatures of imitation in many areas of life, following the

example of others for good or ill. Too many people in the public eye—politicians and pop stars, footballers and other sports personalities, prominent figures from all aspects of life—frequently set a bad example. The attitude is built up, 'If they can do it, why can't I?' Thankfulness is caught as well as taught, and example is still the best precept.

Let us return to the simplicity of thankfulness! The saintly Andrew Murray said, 'To be thankful for what I have, and for what my Lord has prepared, is the surest way to receive more'!

I'll never forget a lovable but eccentric Lancashire pastor, I knew long ago. Old-fashioned as the hills, yet tailor-suited to his generation, odd yet mod, holy yet down to earth, laughable yet one you would trust, an embarrassment so often yet a warm, caring soul—I have rarely met a better one.

He had a large congregation – 150, very big for the 1940–1950s—and one mid-week evening the meeting was packed. The prayer meetings were better attended in Pentecostal circles in those days than the Sunday night services! But somehow the chorus singing was not going with the zip, the praise, the joy, the thoughtfulness and devotion that this spiritually perceptive pastor thought it should. So abruptly he raised his hand, stopping all and sundry – pianist, musicians, the whole congregation just ground to a halt, midway through the singing of 'Give me oil in my lamp, keep me burning . . .' He soon drowned the last 'groaners' who had not obeyed his command with a hefty declaration that 'you have little oil tonight, less joy and NO FIRE AT ALL!' Then he ordered everyone out of the building and onto the streets outside! The shocked congregation piled out, with the blustering yet calm white-haired old pastor following behind. He shut the door with a bang, produced a large key from his pocket and promptly locked it.

Standing with his back against the door and facing the amazed congregation blocking the narrow street outside, he announced that there would be no meeting till they obeyed the Word of the Lord – and he produced his large black Bible and read loudly, so that the whole neighbourhood could hear, 'Enter his gates with *thanksgiving* . . . and his courts with praise . . .' You have not done that. When you are truly thankful to the Lord and have lost your apathy and coldness of soul and come truly praising the Lord, I will open the door and we will enter His house with a holy attitude!'

Soon they were singing choruses lustily with hands raised and a more prayerful spirit entered their hearts. Awakened out of slothfulness they began to feel God in the heart, to really show him their love, really touch him in their spirit, and adoration and praise swept the street! Glory and joy and awe and love and thankfulness rose from their inner most beings. After twenty minutes or half an hour, the old pastor gently unlocked the door and the congregation entered with grateful hearts—and what a meeting it was! The old pastor never had to teach them that lesson again!

There is a little PS to that story. A few miles away in a branch church belonging to this congregation, a very young pastor who was a protégé of the old man heard what had happened in the parent church. He was holding a week-night meeting a few days later, and the 15 people who gathered did not seem to be worshipping with much exaltation and victory. So he tried the same tactic as his old father-in-the-faith. He promptly ordered everyone out, locked the church door, gave a lecture outside and a prayer, but when he looked up after his intercession there was no one left – they had all gone home! And the story goes that they never came back! We must be grateful and have a praising heart, but people cannot be forced into such an attitude!

Shakespeare's King Lear cried, 'How sharper than a serpent's tooth it is to have a thankless child . . .' Paul spoke of those who 'when they knew God, glorified him not as God, neither were thankful' (Romans 1:18–21). Shakespeare wrote that the winter wind is 'not so unkind as man's ingratitude.' Among the list of sins of the flesh in 2 Timothy 3:2 is being 'disobedient to parents, unthankful . . .' Browning wrote, 'Lips cry,

God be merciful . . . who ne'er cry, God be praised!' How sad it is to see nothing to be thankful for. The magnetic power of gratitude is irresistible . . . for even in heaven we shall be giving 'thanks to him that sat on the Throne', and we shall cry to him, 'Blessing, and honour and wisdom and thanksgiving . . .' (Revelation 4:9; 7:12).

I'll never forget the man in St George in Bristol, where I held a mission some years ago. He had been a beautiful violonist but had lost his sight, and had not played for many years. In those marvellous meetings that shook the east side of Bristol, with scores converted and many finding miraculous healing, his eyesight was restored. The next time I visited that church he was at the front with the musicians, a radiant smile on his face playing his violin for the glory of God. How he gave a big 'thank you' to God for his restoration to full health.

3. *Speech*. Many have betrayed themselves, hurt themselves, carried wounds for a lifetime, had eternal regrets because of words spoken 'out of season'. When the people of Israel grumbled, Moses said, 'the Lord heard the voice of your words' (Deuteronomy 1:34). Jesus warned, 'By thy words thou shalt be justified, and by thy word thou shalt be condemned.'

Remember the verse:

A careless word may kindle strife;
A cruel word may wreck a life;
A bitter word may hate instil;
A brutal word may smite and kill.

In the words of the poet:
If your lips would keep from slips,
Five things observe with care –
Of whom you speak, to whom you speak,
Of how, and when and where

The manner of our words and the way in which they are uttered may cause unnecessary pain. I often pray for myself as well as others, 'O Lord, free me from idle and wrong and careless and colourless words and speech.'

Catherine Bramwell Booth wrote, 'The tongue is like the mint that creates coins. It can turn out base, devalued coinage of little or no value, stamped with the sign of the earthly and wordly – or coins of pure gold bearing the image of the divine!'

Be careful, much more is gained by sweet, gentle, thoughtful words, as Lincoln said: 'A drop of honey catches more flies than a gallon of a gall.' Do not speak hurtful, hard, relentless words. Be of simple, honest speech, use words of integrity and purity. Do not use your tongue to gossip or criticise. 'Thy tongue deviseth mischiefs; like a sharp razor working deceitfully,' said David of an enemy.

If I had not vowed not to speak against or criticise others, I am sure God would not have blessed me with spiritual prosperity and a miraculous ministry.

Many notable characters in history have commented on the foolishness of criticising.

- John Wanamaker: 'I learned years ago it is foolish to criticise or scold – I have enough of my own limitations, without fretting over the fact God has not seen fit to distribute evenly the gift of intelligence . . .'
- Abraham Lincoln's favourite text: 'Judge not, that ye be not judged.'
- Confucius: 'Don't complain about the snow on your neighbour's roof, when your own doorstep is unclean.'
- Benjamin Franklin: 'I will speak ill of no man . . . and speak all the good I know of everybody.'
- Dr Johnson: 'God himself does not propose to judge man until the end of his days. Why should I?'

Speak kind, gentle, good words. Strengthen, uplift, cheer others by your statements. We need to lay our tongue on God's altar and ask him to give us power to control, cleanse, hold it, bridle it, sweeten it and speakforth words of blessing, positiveness, joy power, healing, inspiration and faith. Fill your heart and mouth with faith words, power words, life-generating words

. . . 'Death and life are in the power of the tongue,' says the proverb. Use your tongue rightly, blessedly, faithfully, joyfully. Speak anointed words, light-bearing words, life-charging words. For

> A gracious word may smooth the way;
> A joyous word may light the day;
> A timely words may lessen stress;
> A loving word may heal and bless.

4. *Awe and wonder*. Awe, reverence, fear of God have little place in men's hearts today. Yet the Scripture says we need to fear God. 'Let the earth fear the Lord, let all the inhabitants of the world stand in awe of him' (Psalm 33:8).

'My heart standeth in awe of thy word. I rejoice at thy word' (Psalm 119: 161–2).

'Stand in awe . . . commune . . . be still . . . trust in the Lord . . .' (Psalm 4:4–5).

When Bredan the Anglo-Saxon evangelist was seeking to convert one of the early kings of Britain in Wessex, the king asked, 'If I become a Christian what will I receive?'

Bredan replied, 'O king, nothing but wonder, upon wonder, upon wonder . . .'!

We need to keep a sense of wonder at the majesty of God. As Tozer said, 'Nothing deforms and twists the soul more than a low or unworthy conception of God.'

Paul spoke of the transforming power of gazing on our Lord: 'But we all, with open face beholding as in a glass the glory of the Lord, are changed into the same image from glory to glory, even as by the Spirit of the Lord' (2 Corinthians 3:18).

As we gaze on him, the drabness, staleness, dullness of living is replaced by living that has freshness and glory What a way to live!

I like the verse about wonder transforming people in Betjeman's poem about the couple he spied in a Bath tea shop:

She, such a very ordinary little woman:
He, such a thumping crook:
But both, for a moment, a little lower than the
angels
In the tea shop inglenook.

5. *Friendships.* Watch your contacts and friendships. The people we mix with, we become like.

God has great plans for us. He wants to make us like Jesus. 'For those whom God had already chosen he also set apart to become like his Son' (Romans 8:29, TEV). If this is to be accomplished we must have fellowship with Jesus. We achieve this by walking with him. 'If we walk in the light (God's Word), as he is in the light, we have fellowship one with another, and the blood of Jesus Christ his Son cleanses us from all sin (1 John 1:7). His companionship will transform us and it will be said of us as it was said of the Apostles, 'The members of the Council were amazed to see how bold Peter and John were and . . . they realised that they had been companions of Jesus (Acts 4:13). Furthermore, Christians are promised, 'When Christ appears we shall be like him' (1 John 3:2). The sons of men will resemble the Son of God.

Do not linger in the enemy's city – like Lot!
Do not warm your hands by the enemy's fire – like
Peter!
Do not sleep in the enemy's lap – like Samson!
Do not die an enemy's death, as fool dies – like
Abner!

Success rises and falls according to relationships. Find friends whose hearts are set on the holy pilgrimage. Stanley Jebb said, 'You cannot drive 10-ton trucks over plywood bridges . . .' Build stone foundations, good relationships, sound friendships forge bonds that can take the weight of growth, success, pressures, demands, troubles, so that you have others to help you bear the burdens of the work.

6. Self-Surrender

There is an old Chinese story of two men walking along the riverside one day, when suddenly they hear a cry from a man struggling in the river, and it is quite clear that he is drowning. One of the chinese said to the other, 'I cannot help him, I cannot swim, but you are a strong swimmer!' The other said nothing about the drowning man, but just continued with his original conversation. The drowning man went down the first time, then came up screaming. The man on the bank who could not swim looked much concerned, saying to his friend, 'Are you not going to save him?' The other man ignored the drowning man and his plea and just went on walking and talking about other things. The man in the river came up screaming a second time, but no response came from the strong swimmer on the bank. As he went down for the third and fatal last time, as the water gurgled above him, suddenly the man on the bank threw off his garment and dived into the water. The other man watched wide-eyed from the riverside as the strong swimmer pulled the drowning man out of the water and soon had him on the bank, pumping water from his lungs. Before long he was sitting up recovering.

The man who had watched everything said to the lifesaver, 'Why did you leave it till the very last second before saving him?'

And the man replied, 'I waited till he stopped struggling.'

God is waiting for our self-surrender, until we stop fighting, stop struggling, stop arguing with him. It is for us to yield. Bonhoeffer said, 'When Christ calls a man, he bids him to come and die!' He is looking for broken, submissive, surrendered, yielded vessels

I was once in a great meeting with Corrie ten Boom. She only spoke for a few minutes, and virtually said the same thing over and over again, but she left something behind deep in our hearts, perhaps more than those who preached for two hours! She kept saying in her quiet Dutch voice: 'There is only one way forward with the Master – surrender, surrender, surrender.'

Four aspects of self-surrender are:

1. Take spiritual truth in deadly earnest, seriously seek God and his will for you.

2. Throw yourself recklessly upon God. Surrender all to him, put all your ambitions, plans and possessions into his hands.

3. Let God have all honour in your life. Take a solemn vow never to steal or share in the glory and praise which belong to him.

4. Make up your mind not to defend yourself against persecutors, detractors, Judases or any untrue statements made against you by jealous Christians or ministers. This is a tough and rugged way, but it is the only way to enjoy the inner deeper life that is in Christ. I have sought to follow this ideal closely over the past few years and have never enjoyed such a magnificent harvest of blessing, prosperity, joy, power, miracles and soulwinning. It is costly, but it is the way to revival!

Dr Sangster called self-surrender 'Making Christ truly King – not president who only rules for a while – but King who rules over you.

Paul expressed it best of all: 'I am crucified with Christ: nevertheless I live; yet not I, but Christ liveth in me: and the life which I now live in the flesh I live by the faith of the Son of God, who loved me, and gave himself for me.'

With vision undimmed, a thankful spirit, guarded speech, awe and wonder, right friendships and complete surrender, we are ready to meet the King and we have boundless bountiful LIFE!

11: *Get Wisdom*

Almost all problems arise from lack of wisdom. Most church problems are due a lack of wise handling by the minister – he is not always the source of the problem, more often than not he isn't, but his unwise dealing with situations increases the problem.

Wisdom, someone said, is 'making less wrong decisions than right ones', or 'doing the right thing at the right time'. I've seen businesses lost, churches closed, good men heading for disaster, families broken up, youth going astray, all through lack of wisdom. Someone described wisdom as 'an inclination toward right decisions of life'.

The Scripture extols the value of wisdom. King Solomon chose wisdom rather than riches. He tells us in Ecclesiastes: 'The words of wise men are heard in quiet more than the cry of . . . fools. Wisdom is better than weapons of war . . . The words of a wise man's mouth are gracious.'

In Camberley, England, there is a world-famous college which many prospective generals, admirals, air marshals, presidents and leaders of nations attend. It was founded over 150 years ago with the vision that all soldiers need to be taught leadership, and no British officer can attain command until he has successfully completed this course. The college symbol is an owl, and its motto is *Tam Marte Quam Minerva,* which, roughly translated, means *War Needs Wisdom*. It is the Army Staff College located in the grounds of the Royal Military Academy, Sandhurst. Again and again throughout their time spent there, students are urged to formulate their aim, to define it precisely: to know where they are going and why. This is done at the strategic level, putting broad detail into those plans. To learn wisdom is vital if they are to succeed.

Many great Bible men urged us to find wisdom. Paul urged, 'Walk in wisdom.' James described it, 'The wisdom from above is first pure, then peaceable, gentle, and easy to be intreated, full of mercy and good fruits, without partiality, and without hypocrisy.' Solomon's experience was, 'Happy is the man that findeth wisdom . . . My son . . . keep sound wisdom and discretion'. No wonder Job said, 'The price of wisdom is above rubies.'

Let's face it, life is full of problems. Many things that happen we cannot understand and never will in this life. However, because we do not know the answer to a perplexing situation, it does not mean there is no answer. It may well be that God in his infinite love deems it wise to hide some things from us on occasions because this is to our advantage. I wonder if, in our present state, it would contribute to our happiness if we knew what he knows?

Whereas knowledge is useful, it also can lead us to problems as we in this space age well know. Our greatest need is not more knowledge, but wisdom. It would be wiser for us at times to be content with the knowledge that God knows all the facts and that he has the solution to that which seems at the moment a mystery.

Our existence may be compared to a work of art on tapestry. At the moment, what we gaze upon may appear to be meaningless, a tangled mess of broken or loose threads in various colours; a complex jigsaw conveying little. But when we get to Heaven we will behold the other side of the handiwork. Then will be revealed a glorious pattern of magnificent design. We shall see the finished work of incomparable artistic beauty woven by the divine hand. This will be the day of revelation, as Paul says in 1 Corinthians 13:12 (Phillips): 'At present all I know is a little fraction of the truth, but the time will come when I shall know it as fully as God now knows me!'

James says we can expect all kinds of trials and temptations as we go through life. We may have experiences that will leave us nonplussed, but 'If, in the process, any of you does not know how to meet any particular problem he has only to ask God . . . and he may be quite sure that the necessary wisdom will be given him' (James 1:5, Phillips).

Many Christians will readily testify to receiving a word of wisdom from God after earnest prayer. Sometimes he inspires his people to take a firm line of action to solve a difficulty, or we may be led to be still and let God work out a problem in his time.

Occasionally he may give us the ability to perceive that a particular issue will not be fully solved here and that we should leave the matter is his hands. Wisdom sees beyond time to the day when all things will be worked out according to his eternal purpose and to our satisfaction.

Every time we seek life, fulfilment, peace, achievement for God, we shall be challenged by the powers of darkness! We shall need wisdom to live life to the full, to advance, to have joy and a full family life.

A survey of missionaries, some who had laboured successfully for some time in needy Third World countries, showed that of those who gave up and returned home, in 75 per cent of the cases it was due to being unwise in interpersonal relationships. Lack of wisdom drove many talented, gifted and badly-needed people to give up and go home failures!

I have seen a man of God demonstrate great power and promise—then *he blows it* by overstepping the mark!

I have seen a promising marriage end in tatters through indiscreet actions. Wisdom would have saved them!

Jim Williams, pastor of possibly the largest church in New Zealand, made a comment one day during a campaign when we were enjoying a meal together – a beautiful 'Kiwi' pavlova! He said that the special gift or anointing we have from God is like an electric cable. The cable carries millions of volts of great power, which would all be unharnessed without the insulation of the cable. In the same way, wisdom is the insulation to God's gifts, abilities and powers in a man or woman.

How true, the greater the power and abilities and potential and blessings in a life, the greater the need for wisdom to handle it. In a lightning storm, think of all the power that lights up the sky – electricity all over the place, impressive, even magnificent to watch, powerful, but *useless*. It occasionally even destroys people and buildings, because it has no cable, no harnessing, no insulation!

In the same way, without wisdom we lose our undeveloped spiritual powers.

Dr J. H. Jowett said in one of his sermons that botanists had discovered that the soil of England contained numerous seeds of tropical plants from the most remote regions of the earth. They were brought here by the birds and the winds. It was the theory of one renowned botanist that given ten months of tropical warmth the land would be covered with flowers of tropical variety and luxuriance. In our lives, too, there are undeveloped powers which are God-given. They are awaiting the right spiritual temperature to come forth and serve in the cause of God.

They await wise channelling! So you see, without wisdom, all is lost. *Seek wisdom . . .*

What's inside of you determines whether you achieve the peak in your life. With wise handling your life can achieve its full potential.

This interesting verse came into my hands some years ago:

What Kind are You?
The *unwise* are like *wheelbarrows* . . .
no good unless pushed.
Others are like *kites* . . .
if you don't keep a string on them, they fly away.
Others are like *kittens* . . .
they are more contented when petted.
Others are like *footballs* . . .
you can't tell which way they will bounce next.
Others are like *balloons* . . .

full of hot air and ready to blow up.
Others are like *neon lights* . . .
they keep going on and off.

But others let the Holy Spirit guide them with his wisdom, and are like a good watch – open faced, pure gold, quietly busy and full of good works.

Wisdom enables us to handle difficult problems, and the relationships that would destroy our peace and hinder contented living.

Here are three ways to develop wisdom.

1. *Centralise Christ.* The more we think of him, follow him, soak our hearts and minds in his Word, the more we gain in wisdom.

Frank Salisbury, the portrait painter, used to tell a story of a young art student, who always wanted to draw a portrait of Christ, but felt he could never do so. He went to the trenches in the First World War and while billeted in France with many other men, he noticed many vulgar drawings pinned above the beds. Then he remembered his old desire to paint Christ. He worked at night by the flicker of a candle, and when he had finished he put it above his bed. No one laughed or cursed, it was met with silence. But over the next day or two without a word every single obscene picture was taken down by the men themselves. Only the face of Christ remained on the wall.

All the attractions of the world, its pleasures, its sins, its materialism, pale into nothing compared with the peace, power, joy and life that Jesus gives.

2. *Learn positiveness.* This encourages wisdom and wise actions. I never met a depressive or pessimist who had great wisdom. The wise man is one who takes risks, who has faith, who always expects the best from God and out of situations.

Fifty years ago thousands of Sunday School children became 'Sunbeams'. This was their pledge:

I will talk health instead of sickness;
I will talk prosperity instead of failure;

I will carry good news instead of bad news;
I will tell cheerful stories instead of sad ones;
I will mention blessings instead of my burdens;
I will speak of the sunshine instead of the clouds;
I will think of the cheerful things, not the gloomy,
and my thoughts will shine in my face;
I will praise . . . those making . . . honest effort to
perform their tasks . . .
I will always remember a merry heart doeth good like
medicine!

3. *Wisdom grows by daring*. Winston Churchill said in his book about painting that when you approach the easel with palette and brush, the canvas seems to look up at you and say, 'You dare!' And it is the same with wisdom. Each day we are challenged to hazard our lives in the service of Christ. We learn by *risking*, by winning and losing. We grow in maturity by trying, daring, working out our vision, taking leaps into the dark – *risking* – and then come out stronger, bolder, wiser. And if we lost or did not gain by our daring, we learned how not to do it next time!

- Gideon dared everything as he cut his army down to 300 in the face of a great enemy but he dared to believe and risk everything on God's promises.
- Abraham dared everything as he took his son up to slay him and offer him as a sacrifice . . . but God was true to his own character and blessed him.
- Elijah dared everything as he boasted before the pagan priests of Baal that his God was true and would light the soaking wooden altar . . . God answered with fire!

Oscar Wilde declared that 'an idea that is not dangerous is hardly worth calling on'! No daring – no wisdom gained. Seize opportunities, take advantage of them. There's never a shortage of new things to learn and people to help. As Teddy Roosevelt said, 'Far better it is to *dare mighty things* . . . even though checkered by some failures than rank with those poor spirits who enjoy neither victory nor defeat . . .'

Through wisdom we

—uncover great opportunities
—discover beautiful solutions
—overcome impossible obstacles
—unwrap surprises God has in store
—roll back dark clouds until the sunlight breaks through.

What's holding you back? Be wise and see:

a goal you should be pursuing
a dream you should be launching
a plan you should be executing
a project you should be starting
a possibility you should be exploring
an opportunity you should be grabbing
an idea you should be working
a problem you should be tackling
a decision you should be making

John Masefield, the former British Poet Laureate, wrote:

Sitting still and wishing
Makes no person great
The good Lord sends the fishing
But you must dig the bait . . .

Be willing to dig! *Dare*!

There is another kind of wisdom, which is beyond the wisdom which we can develop through godly living and spiritual maturity. It is the Word of Wisdom, which is a supernatural gift, one of the nine gifts of the Holy Spirit, granted by him alone.

Many times I have known this gift operate in my life and ministry. It works with its partner gift the gift of Word of Knowledge. God shows me something about a person, or gives me an insight or warning about circumstances, people or certain actions . . . then the Gift of Wisdom operates and I know what to do in those circumstances.

Chapters 16 and 17 in John's Gospel reach the highwater mark of the teaching of Jesus about the Holy Spirit. The Holy Spirit was active of course before the day of Jesus. The Old Testament makes it abundantly clear that great works of wisdom or craftsmanship, the art of the ruler, the work of the prophets, were all part of the inspiration of the Spirit.

The emphatic teaching of the New Testament is that the Christian religion is supernatural. Christians are supernaturally born again, the Christian life is supernatural. In these verses Jesus says that the Holy Spirit would help people to understand his teaching. It is important to remember that Christian truth does not come by scholarship alone but through the Holy Spirit of God. He is called the Spirit of truth. Reason can investigate the facts, explore phenomena, classify, knowledge, certify evidence and the rest. The Spirit goes deeper and illuminates truth. There are certain truths that cannot be known by any other means than the way of revelation. Christian wisdom cannot be discovered by human intellect; and intelligence which is unaided cannot discern the deep things of God.

It is only through the Spirit of Jesus invading human life that Christians can speak with authority. It is by the Spirit that we have the joy of assurance, the gift of peace, the endowment of power, the efficiency of service.

The most important factor, is that, through the Holy Spirit, God comes to dwell in us. God is both the Gift and the Giver. He is our source of love, our source of power – and our source of wisdom too.

'If any of you lack wisdom, let him ask of God . . . and it shall be given him' (James 1:5).

'Christ . . . in whom are hid all the treasures of wisdom' (Colossians 2:3).

'I will give you a mouth and wisdom,' said Jesus (Luke 21:15).

'The fear of the Lord is the beginning of wisdom' (Psalm 111:10).

It certainly is essential for us to possess wisdom if we want to live a spiritually contented life, unhampered by a fog of uncertainties. Note carefully then that we are not only invited to ask for wisdom, but also promised that it will be given liberally in any given situation. Look again at these verses in James chapter 1.

'If any of you lack wisdom, let him ask of God, that giveth to all men liberally, and upbraideth not; and it shall be given him. But let him ask in faith, nothing wavering. For he that wavereth is like a wave of the sea driven with the wind and tossed. For let not that man think he shall receive any thing of the Lord.'

The sad thing is that very few of us ask God for this great spiritual gift, which we so badly need and which he is so ready to give. The Kingdom of God is at the fingertips of the wise!

12: *Patience is The Key*

'I waited patiently for the Lord; and he inclined unto me, and heard my cry' (Psalm 40:1).

Despite the marvels of science and the speed of modern civilisation, we are still called upon to wait. But we are impatient of any delay.

A car stalls at the traffic lights, and within seconds other cars are blasting their horns. That new model capable of reaching sixty miles per hour in ten seconds has to wait. Frustration! Yet waiting is part of life itself.

We see it in nature. The farmer sows his seed and waits for the harvest. Not like a friend's daughter who when she was quite young just couldn't wait, but dug her seeds up after a few days to see if they were growing! We see it in human life: childhood, adolescence, manhood and womanhood. In romance too. A line of a popular song some years ago stated, 'She is worth waiting for'.

And in God's economy, spiritually, waiting is necessary. It is just as much a part of God's plan as that which appears more active and effective. Without waiting is no growth, maturity or fruit.

The saying 'Rome was not built in a day' has more in it than is realised at first glance. The obvious point of the statement is that it takes time and toil and perseverance to do anything of lasting value.

Most people have a desire to achieve something in life. There is a built-in ambition in us all to get on and to be successful. This is seen from a very early age. The little child shows his mother his first attempts at drawing. To him the scribbles and blotches are a masterpiece. His desire to be accepted and acclaimed is clear when he hands his 'Picasso' to his mother for approval.

A burning desire for accomplishment is aroused in the hearts of the young, after watching someone perform an outstanding feat or hearing a celebrated person's exploits. Sometimes the fires of ambition are sparked when we read of the noble achievements of some dedicated man or woman.

But how many of us never get any further than a spur-of-the-moment resolution? Some retire into a world of fantasy and build dream castles rather than face up to the challenge and realities of life. Sometimes we make feverish and spasmodic attempts to go ahead and do something worthwhile and then enthusiasm dies away because we lack what it takes to emulate those we admire.

The first thing that invariably happens to anyone who has visions of accomplishment is to run into difficulties. To give up here is disastrous. We fail to understand that these are the very things that can help a man to succeed.

Disraeli once said, 'Difficulties constitute the best education in life.' H. G. Wells said some goods things in his time. Here is one gem: 'What on earth would a man do with himself if something did not stand in his way?' Let us accept that opposition is inevitable once we start out to conquer the world and it is this that makes life exciting.

One of the main ingredients for success is something that we all know too well and ignore too often. It is so obvious that we tend to over-look it or foolishly dismiss it as unimportant. It is the rare virtue of patience. The old saying goes something like this, 'patience is a virtue, possess it if you can, found seldom in a woman and never in a man.' I think this might be fairly near the truth!

The fact is that unless we possess it then we shall never be truly successful. You can never be a Michelangelo unless you are prepared to chip away at the marble year after year. You will never become a Caruso unless you are determined to exercise and practise your scales long hours, days and months.

No one can get to the top of his or her world without this quality. Ask the successful orators, business tycoons, musicians, politicians, and they will tell you that you cannot succeed without patience.

How true it is also that we need to exercise patience if we hope to change men and women for the better. The Scriptures abound with stories of people who waited. We've already quoted from Psalm 40: 'I waited patiently for the Lord; and he inclined unto me, and heard my cry.' This verse tells us of one who waited, how he waited, and the result of his waiting. Let's look first at what David did, and then at what the Lord did.

David says 'I waited'. He waited in trouble. Verse 2 tells us he was in a horrible pit, in the miry clay. It seems to have been an old decayed cistern or reservoir out of which the water had seeped, leaving it just a slimy pit. He was in darkness, enclosed by those slimy walls, his feet in the mud; and alone. Life without God can be like that. I'm reminded of a man who when he was saved and healed said, 'I was in a pit, many times I struggled up the walls only to fall back further in.'

The margin of my Bible calls it a pit of noise. How descriptive of these days when the din and noise of this modern world can press in upon us, not to mention the disquiet which can arise from within. To be alone isn't necessarily to be quiet.

It's natural to struggle, to try to get out when we are in trouble, but the greater the effort the deeper we sink in the mud. A woman recently told me 'I am frustrated, I can't go forward, I can't go back, what shall I do?' My reply was, 'Stay where you are.' In Isaiah 30 the Lord said to Israel, when they were making every effort to get out of their predicament, 'Their strength is to sit still.'

David waited, but notice how he waited: patiently. In the Epistle of James it is recorded that the prophet Elijah prayed earnestly that it might not rain. The margin says, 'In his prayer, he prayed.' The margin in the Psalm says, 'In waiting, I waited.' There is praying and 'praying'. There is waiting and 'waiting'. There came a time when David ceased to struggle in that mud, to clutch feverishly at those slimy walls, when all the striving went out of his soul, and he waited patiently.

Many folk wait, but not patiently. I was queuing in the fish and chip shop recently, and the fellow in front of me began drumming his fingers on the counter and sighing deeply. He evidently felt there was unnecessary delay, that no one seemed concerned, least of all the man in charge of the business standing by the frier with his hands on his hips. Maybe he had a family waiting at home. I don't know, but one thing was clear: he was mighty impatient.

The Christian Church needs not only compassion for the lost and outcasts of society, but patience to pray and believe and encourage them on the right road.

One day someone asked Susannah Wesley how she could have patience to teach a child the same thing 20 times over. 'Why,' she said, 'If I had stayed at only 19 times, and given over, I should have lost my labour. It was the twentieth time that fixed it.'

Recently I read a paragraph about the history of missions which teaches the same lesson. In western Africa it was 14 years before one convert was received into the church; in South Africa 10 years; in New Zealand, 9 years before there was one baptism; in Burma, Dr Johnson laboured 7 years before he had one convert; and in Tahiti it was 16 years. Yet it is remarkable that in most of these missions where the Gospel was peculiarly tried at the beginning, the success has been most rich and abundant afterwards.

On one occasion I was pioneering and having a difficult time with little encouragement when I had a letter from a fine church pioneer, Clifford Beasley. This charismatic minister established four excellent churches, which are all thriving in England today. He wrote, 'Do not worry about the wet blankets, have enough *fire to dry them out*! Keep on, persist, keep the fire burning.'

We need also to remember that to make a success of our Christian life we are exhorted to 'possess your soul in patience'. This is not the patience that the stoics of the first century advocated, a kind of doggedness and obstinacy, a will hardening itself into flint. Christian patience is not stubbornness, it is not indifference it is not fighting through by sheer determination, it is a patience that is of faith. It is submissive, not of constraint, but willingly. It is the resignation of the whole man to the word and faithfulness of God. It is the serenity of the soul amidst the fiercest of storms as well as in the brightest day of sunshine and happiness.

The New Testament is full of exhortations urging believers to be patient. None perhaps offers a more striking challenge to the Christian to make a complete success of his calling than the words of James 1: 4: 'Let patience have her perfect work, that ye may be perfect and entire, wanting nothing.'

To be successful in the Christian life is surely the aim of all true Christians. To be 'perfect and entire, wanting nothing' means to possess a fully developed character or to arrive at spiritual maturity. For this to take place we are urged to exercise patience in the face of affliction, says James. This seems to be the most difficult of all tests to be endured. But it is through suffering, perhaps more than anything else, that this development takes place. I have witnessed it many times.

Be patient. David waited seven and half years in Hebron. He was 31 years of age in the prime of life and had plenty of time to assert himself, but he not lift a finger to take the throne by force, but patiently waited.

Expectant, patient waiting is always rewarded. George Sumnock said, "To lengthen my patience is the best way to shorten my troubles.' Be patiently persistent . . . you will always win. Paul said, 'Support the weak, be patient toward all men' (1 Thessalonians 5:4)

Joshua and Caleb persisted patiently with faith in God and got into the Promised Land. Millions of Israelites did not persevere and their carcasses littered the desert!

Ruth said to Naomi, 'whither thou goest, I will go,' and persevered and walked into Bible history. But Orpah did not persevere and in reality said, 'Where thou goest, I cannot go'—and walked out of Bible history!

The Romans had a saying: 'Where there is no easy way, we will find one or build one.' Determination, dedication, intention, daily saying 'I will not quit!'

An experiment was conducted in a large steel mill. A giant half-ton bar of steel was suspended by a strong cable. Near it a tiny cork from a bottle was hung by a slender string and made to swing back and forth gently but steadily so that with each swing it tapped against the steel bar. The huge steel bar was closely monitored to see if it showed any effects from the tapping of the tiny bottle cork. It looked ridiculous.

After 5 minutes, there was no effect, after 10 minutes, still no effect, the same after 20 minutes, 35 minutes. But after 50 minutes, amazingly, the great bar began to swing.

At times we can feel like the tiny bottle cork. Our lives may seem insignificant, our labours seem unnoticed, ineffective, our hard work unavailing. But God says, 'He that goeth forth and weepeth, bearing precious seed, shall doubtless come again with rejoicing bringing his sheaves with him' (Psalm 126:6).

'Let us not be weary in well doing: for in due season we shall reap, *if we faint not*' (Galatians 6:9).

A Christian lady who had been lying in bed for some months after an operation asked the doctor one day, 'How long shall I have to be here, doctor?'

He answered cheerfully, 'Oh, only one day at a time.'

The patient was not only comforted for the moment but during the succeeding weeks the thought 'only one day at a time' came back with its quietening influence.

Thank God, he can give us the grace to wait without complaint until deliverance comes and to bear with calmness and without over-eagerness any delay in the accomplishment of our desires. Then when the reward of patience comes it will be sweet indeed.

When we 'wait' for the Lord, we work for it, but do not worry about it! We are patiently determined – but are not lazy or apathetic about it!

13 *Praise-Power*

Praising the Lord has always been for me one of the most inspiring and exalting themes. I love to praise him and hear him praised. I often catch the greatest vision and revelation of God in those indescribable times in our meetings when the atmosphere is electric, the 'roof has come off', and I see the omnipotent King of kings . . .

Where real praise is, there is God. It is like rain to a thirsty field, to be in a torrent of praise to the Almighty.

Baker's *Dictionary of Theology* defines praise as 'homage rendered to God by his creatures in worship of his person and in thanksgiving for his favours and blessings . . .' Praise in various forms is spoken of 550 times in the Bible, many of them in the Psalms. The Jewish religion has what it calls the 'Hallel', Psalms 113 to 118, which are recited 18 times a year in Jewish festivals. Just before the suffering of Calvary Jesus and his disciples would have sung them at the Passover supper and also possibly later in Gethsemane.

Some say, 'I praise God inwardly,' but if there is an abundance of praise in your heart, your mouth cannot help speaking it – God wants us to praise him freely! Praise gives you a new indestructible confidence with God!

'Oh that men would praise the Lord for his goodness, and for his wonderful works to the children of men! For he satisfieth the longing soul, and filleth the hungry soul with goodness' (Psalm 107: 8–9).

It is no particular commendation when we rejoice when things go well for us. But in Acts chapters 4 and 5 when the Church was up against great persecution, much prayer was made, great grace was upon them, and there was abundant praise and rejoicing. Soon they were in a state of peace and everything worked out in victory. Prepare to meet the King in power if you have a praising heart!

Madame Guyon while suffering in the Bastille prison could say, 'O the blessedness of an accepted sorrow and the joy of glad submission . . .' Paul was able to 'glory in tribulation . . . rejoice in hope of the glory of God.' Praise, joy, rejoicing bring us into God's presence and enable Him to bring us through. Hell gives way to praise and prayer.

This is the time to arise and praise the Name of Jesus! This is the time to arise and scatter his enemies! His foes cannot lodge in an atmosphere that is filled with the praises of God. Hallelujah, we rejoice in the King!

One of the lepers Jesus healed 'turned back, and with a loud voice glorified God.' Jesus said to him, 'Arise, go thy way: thy faith hath made thee whole.'

Praise, brings God's saving process into effect into our lives. Praise brings revelation, prepares us for miracles, leads to the triumph of God. The praise way is God's way into God's presence!

Praise does not depend on our feelings, moods, or outward circumstances. As Amie Semple McPherson used to say, 'If you do not feel like praising the Lord, *praise the Lord till you feel like it.*'

In our meetings nationwide and across the world, as we praise the Lord, his power and victory and honour fill the tent, or church, or auditorium. I was near Toulouse, southern France, recently where hundreds packed the auditorium filling every available space. As I finished preaching, 50 were immediately converted. The spirit of praise broke out in an unusual way for this part of Europe. I praised God for healing the people *already*, and for his goodness and mercy to us, and then called for those with crippled conditions to demonstrate their healing. A lady danced in the aisle waving a crutch, a man trotted off his sticks, a blind lady called out she could see the colour of my shirt, deaf folk could soon hear the thunderous applause! Here was praise-power in demonstration. God's power was released, as we magnified the King of kings for all his love, goodness and mercy!

When faced with discouragement, life-sapping miseries, sickness, trouble, misunderstandings, stresses, depressions, *look to Jesus*, praise him with all your heart, and the upward flight of your praises will give you powers you've never known before. Exalt and magnify the lamb for sinners slain, heap up praises, crown him with glory, let your heart be tuned up with rejoicing . . . and then see coldness, self, formality and all these troubles *evaporate*! Praise cannot substitute for prayer. Rather, praise *strengthens* prayer. It produces an attitude of victorious prayer. But also, praise *results* from prayer.

Jesus encouraged us to 'ask, and ye shall receive, that your joy [rejoicing, praise] may be full' (John 17:24). The task of asking has its reward in receiving, and in the praise and joyful witnessing that ensue. The powers of darkness are put to flight by the powerful weapon of praise.

Fix your eyes on him, fill the tabernacle with his praises. Then souls are blessed, human nature transfigured, vessels are filled, revival comes and the latter rain is poured out . . . The desert blossoms as a rose . . . miracles abound.

When Solomon gave his long oration at the dedication of the Temple, nothing happened, but when the people began to praise him the glory cloud filled the temple. The Lord came down in presence and power and great glory!

Praise lifts discouraged hearts, meets problems, gives strength to face life's dilemmas, defeats despair. The success of a praising heart is unimaginable.

It was a dream. A puzzled Christian found himself in a strange and weird place. Before him stood a large building. He tried the door. It opened into what looked like a vast storehouse. Piled on all sides were great sacks, most of them stuffed to bursting. But near the doorway lay one that was almost empty. He was about to investigate when a loud voice startled him; he turned, and found himself face to face with the devil.

'How did you get in here?' was his angry demand.

'I tried the door,' was the Christian's meek reply. 'It was unlocked, so I walked in. Sorry if I trespassed.'

'You've no business here. Don't you know it's private?'

'All right, but I have apologised,' said the man, getting a little bolder. 'Before I go, would you mind telling me what is in all these sacks?'

'No!' roared the devil. Then he hesitated, and continued, 'But since you've seen all this you may as well know the rest. This is my granary. Those sacks are full of seeds that I sow in the hearts of men. What a collection!' He rubbed his hands with glee. 'Oh, what a collection—avarice, malice, spite, falsehood, lust, greed, pride, arrogance, gluttony, laziness—ho! ho! ho!'

'But what of this sack that's almost empty?' enquired the intruder.

'Get out! That's one of my deepest secrets,' replied the devil with great heat.

'But do tell me,' pleaded the Christian as he made for the door.

'You cheeky . . . But hold on. For your impertinence I'll tell you. These are my host useful seeds – seeds of discouragement. I sow them again and again – they seldom fail to spring up. Many a promising field has been blighted by this weed. It's terrific!' The devil's face glowed with evil delight.

'But begone!' he snapped.

'One last thing,' said the intruder. 'Are there any hearts in which these seeds cannot be sown?'

The devil was silent for a moment, then went on: 'You may as well know. I cannot sow the seeds of discouragement in a *praising heart*.'

The dreamer awoke; but he never forgot the lesson.

'Every day will I bless thee; and I will praise thy name for ever and ever. Great is the Lord, and greatly to be praised; and his greatness is unsearchable (Psalm 145:3).

As you praise and magnify God, your spirit will be lifted. Praise will scatter your doubts as the sun scatters the gloom. Adore him unceasingly, for this is the glorious privilege of a Christian.

Jesus was always praising and thanking God. Look at the case of Lazarus. Lazarus, whom he loved, was still in the grave, and Jesus had wept. Then, standing in front of the opened tomb, he said, 'Father, I thank thee that thou hast heard me.'

When he stood alone with his small band of followers, rejected by those he came to redeem, he gave thanks to his father: 'I thank thee, O Father, Lord of heaven and earth . . .'

He went to his agony at the Cross with a psalm of thanksgiving. 'When they had sung an hymn, they went out into the Mount of Olives.' It was probably the great Halleluia Psalm that they sang!

Look at Paul. Among all the apostles none suffered so much as Paul, but none of them do we find so often giving thanks as he. Listen to his exhortation: 'Rejoice, and again I say, rejoice.'

Begin your time of prayer, then, by thanking him for former mercies. We ought to be a lot more thankful than we are for what God gives us. If a mother has a child who is constantly complaining and is never thankful, there is little pleasure in doing anything for such a one. If you met a beggar who was always grumbling and never seemed to be thankful for what you gave him, you would very soon shut the door and refuse to give him anything at all. There is surely no sin more offensive to God, or more common among men, that the sin of ingratitude. He must be deeply grieved by the thanklessness of which many of us are guilty.

There is a lot said in the Bible about praise, as well as about prayer, yet how little we praise God! Whereas David said he would pray to God three times a day, he said that he praised God seven times a day! In his Psalms he always mixes praise with prayer.

As you begin to thank him, many blessings will come to your mind. There are many almost unnoticed benefits that he daily confers on us – sleep, appetite, loved ones, soundness of body and mind are a few.

God is looking for worshippers. This is one of the inner meanings of prayer. Prayer is more than words, for it is mightiest when wordless. It is more than asking, for it reaches its highest glory when it adores and worships and asks nothing.

'Our Father which art in heaven, hallowed be thy name . . .' When the disciples asked Jesus to teach them to pray, our Lord showed that all true prayer must begin with praise and worship. And as he ended the model prayer, he concluded with these words: 'For thine is the kingdom, the power and the glory, for ever. Amen.'

In these sentences Christ revealed a secret of prayer. All prayer that reaches God must begin and end with worship. As creatures before our Creator, we owe God sincere worship and praise. Worship, therefore, is the first element in prayer.

It is right here that some make a mistake. They regard prayer mainly as a means by which they can receive help in a time of emergency. Read John 4:23 and you will see that God is seeking people to *worship* him, not merely to run to him when they are in trouble.

Satan also competes for the worship of man. When the devil tempted Christ he promised him all the kingdoms of this world if he would fall down and worship him (Matthew 4:9). Jesus spurned the offer and told Satan that worship must be reserved for God only.

When little children praised the Lord as he made his triumphal entry into Jerusalem, instead of rebuking them as he was urged to do, he said: 'Yeah, have ye never read, Out of the mouths of babes and sucklings thou hast perfected praise?' (Matthew 21:16).

Praise brings the Baptism of the Holy Spirit. Some people beg and beg for the Holy Spirit and go away empty-handed. Others come praising God, and receive very quickly. It was when the 'trumpeters and singers were as one, to make one sound to be heard in praising and thanking the Lord' that the Temple of Solomon was filled with the glory of God (2 Chronicles 5:13). It was when the disciples were praising and blessing God (Luke 24: 52–3) that the Holy Spirit came and 'filled all the house where they were sitting' (Acts 2: 1–2).

Praise is the key to entering God's presence. 'Enter into his gates with thanksgiving, and into his courts with praise' (Psalm 100:4). If you want something from God, then begin to thank him for what he has already done for you.

It is as we begin to think over his former blessings that praise and thanksgiving will spring up in our hearts. In fact, the words 'think' and 'thank' come from the same root. The more we think, the more we shall thank. Thanksgiving is an essential part of praise.

If you wonder 'What can I thank God for?' begin to thank him for himself. We all take God for granted. We seem to assume that he is ours—ours to be had just when and where he is needed, always at our disposal, always at our beck and call, in spite of our neglect and ill-treatment.

He is at our disposal, but we must thank him for it. Therefore, begin to adore him for just what he is and what he has been to you.

'What is thy Beloved more than another beloved?', ask the bridemaids in the Canticles. And the bride's reply is a poem of adoration as she sings of the bridegroom's beauty. It is his person that she finds so adorable; it is what he is that she adores. We have lost much of the spirit of the Jews and early Christians who could so proudly say, 'In God we boast all the day long.'

The word 'adoration' has been defined as the act of rendering divine honour, including in it reverence, esteem and love. It is literally signifies to apply the hand to the mouth, 'to kiss the hand'; in Eastern countries this is one of the great marks of respect and submission. The importance of coming before God in this spirit is often impressed upon us in the Word of God. It is in adoration that we are united to the service of the holy angels, for they prostrate themselves before the Throne of God, saying: 'Holy, Holy, Holy, Lord God Almighty!' As we abase ourselves before him, the sense of his utter

167

holiness will creep over the soul, and we fall at his feet, confessing his worthiness and our unworthiness.

Adoration is closely akin to worship, or, as the word literally means, 'worth-ship', that which is worthy of honour. 'I will call upon the Lord, who is worthy to be praised . . . O come, let us worship and bow down: let us kneel before the Lord our Maker.' What is worship? It is never a mere asking for gifts, and still less a resolute insistence that we ask shall be given us. It is greater than all this. It is often a devout meditation upon God: on the wonders he has wrought; on the heavens which declare his glory; on the earth, which is full of his goodness, and so on. In a word, it is thinking with God in all our thoughts.

Take Hannah, for instance. She is made joyful by the gift of a man-child, and she simply exults in God. She flings up her whole soul in praise of him who is all in all to her. She asks absolutely nothing for herself or her son, she does not make a single request, and yet her song is a prayer. To God's people in the Old Testament, the worshipping side of prayer was by no means mainly an importunate asking for gifts, but a devout meditation on the character, works and providence of God, and their relationship with him.

Praise is a stand-up extrovert expression. Worship is a deep introvert activity which adores and loves the Father . Bob Gordon said: 'It is the sweet whispers of love through the spirit into the ear of God . . . But praise is like the fitness machine or dumbbells in the Gym, they are the work-outs in God's health centre on the way to a healthy sparkling faith!'

Begin to cry to God, after you have praised and worshipped him first. Even a baby can cry! And a cry brings God to your side! A sincere heartfelt cry will do more than polished phrases and elegant sentences. Tell Jesus you love him. Thank him for dying for you. Say: 'Wonderful Jesus, I praise and adore you.'

As you praise, a hopeful, cheerful buoyancy will take over your spirit. Thank God even for your problems—they may be 'angels in disguise! Thank God you don't know the future—for it means the Lord is still working on it!

Thank him that you have ears to hear, eyes to see, hands to write with. Thank God that Christ lives in you and is loving people through you. Dr Poppen, a great missionary to China for 40 years, after his retirement received a card from a Chinese friend on the fiftieth anniversary of his starting in the ministry. The words he read were: 'We remember you as a mind through which Christ thinks, a heart through which Christ loves, and a hand through which Christ works.' What encouragement!

Praise makes us into a new kind of person. You will thrill to see God's new creation being formed in you.

Find a God worth loving and praising, and you will find a life worth living!

Why then should we praise?

● Jesus began in praise – 'Hallowed be thy name . . .' (Matthew 6:9).

● It is right – 'It is a good thing to give thanks unto the Lord' (Psalm 92:1).

● It is lovely – 'Praise is comely for the upright' (Psalm 33:1).

● It is appropriate – 'Thou art worthy, O Lord, to receive glory . . . for thou hast created all things' (Revelation 4:11).

● It is happy – 'Make a joyful noise unto the Lord, all the earth' (Psalm 98:4).

The value of praise is amazing, the list of its benefits endless. In a church in one town, when the people were bubbling with joy, worshippers of another church complained to the local clergyman, because the 'renewed' Christians were even praising God in the coffee bar afterwards! – To them it seemed inappropriate to praise the Lord outside of the church sanctuary.

Thanks and praise are different. I might say 'thank you' to the milkman for his faithful 4 a.m. call with my 'pinta' through cold winter weather. But I do not praise him. I praise my wife, though, for her good cooking, and for all the loving acts she does for me. The difference is that I have a relationship with my wife, I know her, we adore each other . . .

Praise at its heart is to *know God*. Augustine asked, 'Who can call on thee not knowing thee . . .?' Paul longed 'that I may know him' (Philippians 3:10).

'They that know thy name will put their trust in thee' (Psalm 9:10). When we know him and have a deep relationship with him, our life-style, behaviour, thoughts, standards, speech and whole way of life are a continuous song of praise to him.

'The Lord inhabiteth the praises of Israel' (Psalm 22:3).

'Inhabiteth', '*Yawshab*'in Hebrew, is translated to 'dwell with', 'sit down with', 'remain with', for as a King he is 'enthroned with us'. In praise we enthrone King Jesus, and he dwells with us. He also rules with us, for praise lays the foundation for God's ruling power over us, in us, through us. No wonder it makes for such power in our lives and ministries.

A little boy was told at Sunday School that the way to get prayer answered was to praise God. The little fellow replied, 'Oh, I see, you have to be a creep . . .'!

It's true that if you praise him you'll get good things in your life—it does open the way for answered prayer, healings, miracles. But it's not a matter of having to mollify him, say nice words, or flatter him! Praise is not a key to 'turn God on', or 'curry his favour' or 'soothe his ego'. But praise defeats the atmosphere in which sickness, destruction, fear, futility, discouragement flourish. Praise, Jack Hayford said, 'beats out hell bush-fires'; it releases 'a tornado of holy power which will cast down sin, self, disease and discouragement that Satan has erected'! Praise breathes life into the vacuum death produces on the earth.

Pack plenty of praise into praying and you will put power into it. Thank God for what he has done and for what he is planning to do for you, even if you cannot see it all at the moment. Thank God for the possibilities in your life, for what you can become *through him*. Count your many blessings, thank him for freeing you from guilt, jam your prayers with thankful statements. Fatigue, despair, defeat will evaporate from you!

Satan is allergic to praise. He is neutralised, banned, shaken, chased out by praise. No sermon, seminar, conference, lecture, or book is a substitute for holy praise.

Mighty miracles happen in my meetings when God's people praise him. There were 26 wheelchairs in one meeting in Gorseinon during the great West Wales Revival in 1987, and many stood and walked after the terrific time of praise. Three of the eight nurses who came to bring the sick in a string of ambulances were converted on the spot. The praise was overwhelming!

'Let us offer the sacrifice of praise to God continually, that is, the fruit of our lips giving thanks to his name' (Hebrews 13:15). Say in prayer, 'Lord, things are not going well for me . . . my finances are low, my family has problems, I feel pressures from the top of my head to my shaky knees . . . But you have all the answers. I know you are wonderful. *But answers or not I'm going to praise you.*'

Aimee Semple McPherson, the famous American evangelist of the 1920s, told how as a young woman preacher, widowed with a small child, she tried to hold crusades. Few folk were coming, and she had very little finance to keep her going. On one occasion she could get hardly anyone into her tent meeting, and was about to give up completely, when as she looked out at the half a dozen folk and the rows of empty chairs, she felt she could see the devil laughing at her, crying, 'Failure, failure . . .' She prayed and prayed as she sat on the small platform at the front of the meeting.

Suddenly she saw a host of angels standing side by side all around the tent. They all moved towards her step by step shouting, 'praise the lord . . . praise the lord . . .' Soon they were all around the platform, on the platform, crowding in on her, shouting with a resounding cry, 'Praise the lord!'

She suddenly lit up and joined them, shouting with joy 'Praise him, praise him . . . Praise the Lord . . .' and then they all vanished.

She went on to preach with power that night, and night by night she thanked and praised God. She did not look at circumstances, but worked in the day making the meetings known, praising him all day long. By the end of the week the tent was packed. She went on for weeks, souls were saved, the sick were dynamically cured, miracles happened. She stayed in Los Angeles to build what was to became the largest church in the world prior to the Second World War. Victory through praise! No wonder the Psalmist said, 'Seven times a day do I praise thee . . .'

God is more wonderful than anything the human mind can grasp. If we can catch just a little glimpse of what he is like, we will praise him, and the life of God will flow into us.

Let your praises go up to the King and ring through the decadent atmosphere of earth and into the portals of Glory!

14 *Epilogue: live forever – never die*

I had been holding a successful mission near Llanelli in west Wales. Hundreds had been finding Christ, remarkable miracles of healing had taken place. I was exhausted, and when one of the pastors in charge offered to take me for a ride, I asked to be taken to the boathouse at Lagneharne, home of the famous Welsh poet and writer, Dylan Thomas.

We stood at the river estuary on a bright March day. Spring filled the air, seagulls whined above, the sun shone. Few visitors were there at that time of year, the village was near empty. All was quiet, and the air was sharp and serene.

We made our way to Dylan's grave on a hillside across the lane from the old churchyard. A simple white cross. I remembered his words about death, the thoughts of a chapel boy turned agnostic: 'Do not go gently into that dark night . . .' Words of despair, uncertainty. But as I looked, I almost laughed with delight. For right behind his grave, where thousands of visitors stand during the summer months and quote his poetry, including masses from America where he is very popular, was another grave. On the large white stone was a huge text, which not one of those visitors could miss, bearing the testimony of a man with peace and certainty. It was the declaration of Job: '*I know that my redeemer liveth . . .*'!

I smiled at the hopelessness of Dylan Thomas's belief, and the certainty the Scriptures still present to a modern society. An atheist looked at a lovely sunset and didn't know who to thank! *But the believer knows his God.* 'Because I live, ye shall live also,' promised Jesus.

A little girl was taking a short-cut across a graveyard. It was getting dark, and her friend asked, 'Aren't you afraid to go through there?' She replied, 'Oh no, you see, my home is just beyond the cemetery!' The believer knows where his home is. The Lord said, 'I go to prepare a place for you . . . that where I am, ye may be also.'

Bonhoeffer, imprisoned for standing against Hitler, wrote these immortal words on the eve of his execution: 'Death casts aside all the burdensome claims . . . so at last we may see that which here remains hidden. O freedom, how long we sought after thee . . . Dying, we now may behold thee revealed . . . the Lord . . .'!

Paul called death the 'last enemy'. But for many it is not dying but what may lie over the other side that brings trepidation. John Wesley rode in a cart with a highwayman who was on the way to the scaffold. He asked if he was afraid to die. The man replied, 'I faced death many times on the roads, I am not afraid to die, but I do fear what lies beyond . . .'

Woody Allan humorously expressed his 'non-fear' of death. When asked if he was afraid to die, he replied 'No, I am not, but I don't want to be there when it happens!'

Lee Trevino, the great golfer, when playing at the American Western Open Tournament a few years ago, was struck by lightning and knocked unconscious. He was carried to the clubhouse and regained consciousness, and when questioned by reporters about his experience replied, 'My whole life came up before me, it was awful, I thought I was dead.'

Fear of death is universal. Dr Samuel Johnson declared, 'No rational man can die without uneasy apprehension.' And the famous Duke of Wellington said, 'That man must be a coward or liar who could boast of never having felt a fear of death.' John Huston, the legendary film director who made stars of people like John Wayne and Marilyn Monroe, wrote just before he died a short time ago: 'I don't know where I'm going.'

But we need a prospect for our future.

Bertrand Russell put into words the conclusion and convictions of naturalism and humanism when he said:

'No fire, no heroism, no intensity of thought and feeling can preserve an individual life beyond the grave; that all the labours of the ages, all the devotion, all the inspiration, all the noonday brightness of human genius, are destined to extinction in the vast death of the solar system, and that the whole temple of man's achievement must *inevitably be buried beneath the debris of a universe in ruins.*'

Is there no immortality? Shall we not see our loved ones again? Was the graveside the final and irrevocable farewell? No life everlasting? No heaven? Is there no reunion? Are dust and ashes the goal we are making for? Is there nothing beyond the grave?

A Harvard University professor once lectured on the theme: 'Is eternal existence desirable?' and came to the conclusion that it is not. If all that eternity offers is just existence, who can bear mere existence eternally? But if it's eternal *life* – that's different!

Dr E. Stanley Jones, when referring to the subject of life after death, remarked: 'Only life that is eternal is really life; every other kind of life has the seeds of death in it'.

No Christian need fear that death means extinction, for Christ has said: 'I go to prepare a place for you . . . (John 14:2–3).

Dr W. E. Sangster tells how, as a young boy living in the heart of London, he went for a walk one day and got lost. A kindly policeman took him by the hand and led him to the police station. After waiting for what seemed like several hours in a dingy room, a stern officer came and took him down a dark passage where he saw his father waiting for him. Sangster said, 'It will not be different, I think, when I die. At the end of the dark passage my Father will be waiting.'

Christianity forever sweeps that horror of darkness from our soul and we can stand facing eternity. This is our prospect. This is our peace, our future, our certainty, our hope. Though in the frailty of our human nature we turn away from what some refer to as 'the Grim Reaper', death really has but one mission – to bring us into God's more immediate presence and give us an eternal place in our Father's house.

In the catacombs beneath the city of Rome, where the early Christians hid during the great persecutions of the Church, many drawings and cuttings can be seen sketched on the walls. They include the dove, symbol of the Holy Spirit; the fish, meaning Jesus Christ the Son of God; the peacock, symbolising immortality; and the athlete's victory palm, signifying that we are to be final overcomers. Christ has gained the victory for us, we shall win, we shall finish the course, the believer will be resurrected and will live eternally.

An old legend of the Western Isles tells of a seal king who desired the company of a human being. One day in his cavern under the sea he heard a baby's cry, and he rose to the surface to discover a tiny infant in a derelict boat. Just as he was about to make for the vessel, a rescue party intervened, and he lost his prize. But – so the legend goes – as the boat was towed away, the seal king threw into the heart of the child a little salt wave, saying as he submerged, 'The child is mine. When he grows, the salt sea will call him and he will come home.'

For us, *dying is to find our way home*, to live for ever!

Jesus clearly and uncompromisingly proclaims: 'I am the resurrection and the life. He who believes in me will live, even though he dies; and who ever lives and believes in me will never die' (John 11:25–6, NIV).

A woman was teaching a group of Japanese children on the island of Hawaii about the life and death of Jesus, when one of the children jumped out into the aisle and cried out: 'Ah . . . this is not fair . . . Him one swell guy.' A little girl who knew the story pulled him by the coat-tails and urged him to sit down. 'Don't get upset,' she said. 'He didn't stay dead.'

If he didn't stay dead, nor shall I stay dead.

William James, when asked if he believed in personal immortality, replied, 'Yes – and the more strongly as I grow older.' Why? 'Because I'm just getting fit to live.'

Paul Tillich stated that fear of death is our basic anxiety. I wonder if that is so. Some grow morbid about it; but is there any need to do that?

Said Ellen Terry, calmly and clearly, as she prepared her will in readiness for that moment:

> No funeral gloom, my dears, when I am gone,
> Corpse-gazing, tears, black raiment, grave-yard grimness,
> Think of me as withdrawn into the dimness,
> Yours still, you mine. Remember all the best
> Of our past moments, and forget the rest,
> And so, to where I wait, come – gently – on!

This is the Christian approach to death. When Christ himself drew near to the end of his earthly life, he prepared himself, and those he loved, not for extinction, but for a larger experience. He shed no tears of farewell. And his gallant confidence echoed in the hearts of all who came into a living relationship with Him: 'Be of good cheer, I have overcome the world!'

Donald Hankey was a soldier in the First World War who survived the fierce fighting in the trenches. Just before leading his men into battle, he would put inspiration and hope into them, saying, 'We are going over the top in a minute. If you're hit, it's blighty, if you're killed, it's the resurrection!'

Dr A. J. Gossip had that assurance. He dedicated one of his great books to his wife with these words: 'To Kathryn, long time gone to my Father's house.'

How sad Jean-Paul Sartre's words: 'I came from nothing, I go to nothing, the only happiness is death . . .' How different Dr W. E. Sangster, as he lay dying with muscular atrophy. In a letter to an evangelist friend he wrote, 'All my life I have preached that Jesus Christ is adequate for every crisis. I have but a few days to live, and Christ is indeed adequate in the hour of death. Tell everyone it is true. Tell them from me that God is wonderfully near His children as they come to the end of Life's Road'!

When Ebenezer Erskine became a child of God by faith and was born again, he wrote, 'In the summer of 1702, I got my head out of time into eternity . . .' How important to live with a sense of destiny, of shortness of time, joyfully, yet not lightly, earnestly yet not mournfully, with the glad anticipation that we are going to meet the Lord of Lords.

Hugh Redwood was a Fleet Street sub-editor and a dedicated Christian witness in the 1930–1950s in the hub of newspaper life, in the days when Fleet Street was the centre of world journalism. He described how at end of an exhausting day in a national newspaper office he went to a friend's house. Alone in the room, Hugh noticed a Bible open at Psalm 59, at the words, 'The God of mercy shall prevent me . . .' Then he read that the original Hebrew meant: 'The God of mercy shall meet me at *every corner* . . .' In his exhaustion he realised that meant at death's door also.

How wonderful – he will be with us at the final corner, at the last twist of the road, as we take l'zoff for the heavenly of heavenlies!

William Hunter, a famous doctor, spoke of the truth of this as he lay dying. 'If I had strength enough to hold a pen,' he cried, 'I would write how easy and pleasant a thing it is to die.' Our God in his loving kindness can meet us at every corner, every step of the way. John Oxenham wrote:

> Shapeless and grim
> A shadow dim
> O'erhung my ways
> And darkened all my days,
> And those who saw,
> With bated breath,
> Said, 'Hush! this is death.'

> And I in weakness,
> Slipping towards the night,
> In sore affright

Looked up, and lo, no spectre grim,
But just a dim sweet face.
A sweet, high, mother face,
A face like Christ's own mother's face,
Alight with tenderness and grace.

'Thou art not Death,' I cried,
For life's supreme fantasy
Had never thus envisaged Death to me:
'Thou art not Death – the End.'
In accents winning came the answer, 'Friend,
There is no Death,
I am the Beginning, not the End.'

We may ask the age-old question of David, 'Who may ascend the hill of the Lord? Who may stand in his holy place?' (Psalm 24:3, NIV). The answer is in the Beatitudes – 'the pure in heart, for they will see God . . .' Many long for this.

The Christian faith is the only faith that lights up that dark area of human existence – death. 'And it lights it up,' says Stanley E. Jones, 'not merely with a word, but with a Word become flesh.' Jesus went through the dark experience we call death, and the word of resurrection became flesh in him. Anyone who lives in him is as deathless as he is deathless.

John declared, 'Now this is eternal life: that they may know you, the only true God, and Jesus Christ, whom you have sent' (John 17:3, NIV).

We are going to have a real body, an incorruptible body. The Scripture tells us: 'For we know that if our earthly house of this tabernacle were dissolved, we have a building of God, an house not made with hands, eternal in the heavens . . .'

I was asked for a photo of myself to go with an article I'd written for a Christian magazine. I sent a note saying, 'I shall look much better five minutes after I'm dead – for I will be handsome then – because the Word says that we don't know what we shall be, 'but we know that *we shall be like him* . . .' (1 John 3:2).

God has promised to 'change our vile body, that it may be fashioned like unto his glorious body' (Philippians 3:21)!

Sir Michael Faraday, the famous scientist, when asked 'What are your speculations about the next life?' used to reply, 'I know nothing of speculations, I am resting on certainties'!

A pop singer not long ago suffered the sudden death of his little son. Heartbroken, he was reported as saying, 'All this success and fame – it doesn't mean very much now.' Despair, hopelessness, bitterness instead of certainty.

I remember staying in a household while on a large mission to Shrewsbury, where the young family had been struck with a similar sorrow. Some 18 months before I knew them, they went in to wake their 8-year-old lad up for school one morning, and found him dead on the floor. A fit and healthy child taken for no apparent reason! But as I stayed with them and talked to the family, what a supreme example they were to overcoming faith and devotion to Christ. That loving born-again couple showed the whole of that Shropshire village, their relatives and their business associates that faith in Jesus is sufficient for every situation. *We know* we shall see our loved ones again. The certainty of Christ is the only hope.

Make Selwyn Hughes' great prayer yours:

Lord Jesus, you who are Master of life and death, I am so grateful that in You I see the death of death and the defeat of defeat. In You everything is alive – alive with meaning, destiny, goal – alive for evermore.

O Father, I am so grateful that You are the Centre of my life. Can this life within me die? Never – for it is deathless and immortal. I rest in this glad and glorious assurance. Thank You, Father, Amen.

Derek Prime wrote of his first visit to Chartres Cathedral, renowned for its glorious stained glass window.

Outside, he remarked, one could not see a great beauty in it. But once inside, he looked up through the bleak darkness, and how things changed. As he developed 'new eyes', as the light, shone through, he gazed in wonder at the astonishing beauty of this marvellous window. Through the 'valley of the shadow of death' . . . we shall at least see fully and clearly the immaculate beauty of Heaven, and of our King of kings!

The Bible says Heaven is a 'Kingdom' (Ephesians 5:5), a 'better country' or, literally, a 'fatherland' (Hebrews 11:16), and a 'city' (Hebrews 11:10). Jesus called it 'my Father's house' (John 14:2).

Heaven is mentioned 600 times in the Bible. The Psalmist tells us it is 'high above the earth', and Jesus said, 'I came *down* from heaven . . . I go to prepare a *place* for you.'! A real, literal, genuine place far above the planets and earth, a billion miles away! The Bible says it has gates, trees, walls, streets, rivers, mansions and thrones! A real country. Paul describes it as 'far better' than earth. No wonder Sir Michael Faraday when asked what he would do in heaven said, 'I shall be with Christ and that's enough.'

'And God shall wipe away all tears from their eyes; and there shall be no more death, neither sorrow, nor crying, neither shall there be any more pain: for the former things are passed away' (Revelation 21:4).

I read a biography of Queen Victoria, and learned that she would sometimes go to the slums of London. She went into one home to have tea with an older lady, and when the queen rose to leave, she asked, 'Is there anything I can do for you?'

The woman replied, 'Yes ma'am, Your Majesty, you can meet me in heaven.'

The queen turned to her and said softly, 'Yes, I'll be there, but only because of the blood that was shed on the cross for you and for me.'

Queen Victoria, in her day the most powerful woman in the world, had to depend on the blood of Christ for her salvation. And so do we. The Bible says that God is the Author of peace. God provided salvation through the cross. He made peace by the shedding of his blood. The enmity that exists between you and God can be over quickly, and the peace treaty signed in the blood of his Son Jesus Christ.

No wonder Paul said, 'For me to live is Christ, and to die is gain.' Gain for Paul, because he would see his Saviour face to face. But also, gain for Christ – to have his own child, one for whom he died, in his immediate presence in heaven.

Do you see the death of a Christian like that? Paul's problems was not living or dying, but deciding which was better – Christ here or Christ there?

As one version of that old hymn puts it:

He will keep me till the river
Rolls its waters at my feet;
Then he'll bear me safely over
Made by grace for glory meet.

Paul tells us in 2 Corinthians 3:18 (NIV), 'And we, who with unveiled faces all reflect the Lord's glory, are being transformed into his likeness with ever-increasing glory, which comes from the Lord, who is the Spirit.'

As Charles Wesley wrote:

Changed from glory into glory,
Till in heaven we take our place;
Till we cast our crowns before Thee,
Lost in wonder, love and praise.

Are you becoming more and more like Christ as the days go by? I get so sad to hear those who talk of some experience they had years and years ago, but who have very little of the glory of Christ in their lives now.

Do you long to be stamped with his likeness? Is your Christian life getting better and more wonderful every day? So often we are like a man in a dark room with a candle, when outside is all the glory of the noonday sun.

We are destined for eternity. 'He who began a good

work in you will carry it on to completion until the day of Christ Jesus' (Philippians 1:6, NIV).

How different was the experience of Madame Curie, the great scientist who discovered radium. She went half-demented when her husband died in an accident in Paris, and when the news was brought to her, the great French agnostic cried, 'what shall I do, I have no faith . . . I have no hope . . .'

How different the words of John Wesley, who with joy and a radiant smile said from his death bed, 'the best of all, God is with us . . .'

We have the victory through the living Christ. 'O death, where is thy sting? O grave, where is thy victory?' (1 Corinthians 15:55).

We are going to see the gates of pearl, the streets of gold, breathe the air of an endless paradise, walk the walls of jasper, see the crystal flowing river, stand under the tree of Life, see the garments that are white, the faces bright. We shall sing, shout and shine! We shall be home at the banquet with Jesus the King, face to face forever. No more dangers, no more fatigue, no more suffering, no more hunger, no more slights, no more disappointments, no more graves. No night, all morning, all day . . . the bridal morning of the Lamb!

A boy was studying the piano and practising for his first great recital. He could not get it perfect, and became frustrated, fearing he would be a failure. His mother, a great musician, put her hand gently on his shoulder and quietly assured him: 'Keep at it, do not give up. You can make a mistake in the beginning, you can make mistakes in the middle – the people will forget about them – as long as you *make the end glorious!*'

Yes, you may have made many mistakes in life, had many failures, known many fingers pointed at you . . . but with God in your life, you can persevere and grow and your life can be fully fulfilled. You will not only keep alive all through life but, like the musician, you will *make sure that the end will be glorious!*

A doctor who was a believer was visiting a dying Christian gentleman. As the patient's life ebbed away he had momentary questionings of what heaven was like and was apprehensive.

'What will I find there?' he quietly, weakly, murmured to the physician.

The reply came back 'Do you hear that noise?'

The dying man strained and replied. 'It sounds like scratching.'

The doctor answered.

'Yes, it's my dog. He has never been in this room before. He does not know what it is like in here . . . what is beyond that door he has no idea of . . . but one thing he is *sure* about . . . HIS MASTER IS IN HERE!

'Many things we cannot imagine, but be sure of this,' he whispered. 'JESUS CHRIST OUR LORD AND MASTER IS THERE . . . so all will be well.

Beyond the vale, beyond the door, in the shining city He waits. It will be glorious there. It will be a land fit for heroes.

LIVE LIFE to the full.

KNOW GOD'S POWER FOR LIVING.

OVERCOME THROUGH THE BLOOD OF
    THE LAMB.

KEEP ALIVE IN THE HOLY SPIRIT.

HAVE A FANTASTIC LIFE AND GLORIOUS END.

And say:

'I am convinced that neither death nor life, neither angels nor demons, neither the present nor the future, nor any powers, neither height nor depth, nor anything else in all creation, will be able to separate us from the love of God that is in Christ Jesus our Lord' (Romans 8:38–39).

BELIEVE ON THE SAVIOUR AND LIVE FOREVER!